Contents

Foreword

This short book presents a fresh look at Jews in Scotland over the last two centuries. It is a product of an idea generated by the International Institute for Jewish Genealogy (IIJG) in Jerusalem, whose mission it is to advance Jewish Genealogy as an academic endeavour. To that end, IIJG has sought over the last ten years to broaden the horizons of the research projects it has sponsored. It has, therefore, moved progressively from individual lineages to the family unit, from there to the community or communal framework, and then to a sectoral or regional level.

This expanding focus can be illustrated in some of the studies IIJG scholars have completed, ranging, for example, from Jewish family reconstruction in the Polish city of Piotrków Trybunalski in the nineteenth century, through an examination of kinship networks after the mass emigration westwards of the Jewish community in a small Jewish town (the *shtetl* of Darbenai in Lithuania), to an extended monograph on the lives and lineages of Village Jews in the Russian province (gubernya) of Minsk, where rural Jews made up a quarter and more of the teeming Jewish population there. The challenge to IIJG then became how could Jewish Genealogy be moved to an even broader, or perhaps higher, plane. The logical answer was to try to carry out a genealogical investigation of a national Jewry as a whole, from its inception to modern times, something that, to the best of our knowledge, had never been attempted before.

Scottish Jewry, which emerged as a formal entity in 1816-17, almost commended itself for this experiment. It can be easily demarcated and defined. Its age (200 years old) and size (in the region of 70,000 individuals altogether) make the project feasible. By way of contrast, it would have been impossible to attempt a similar project for the Jewish community of England since the 'Restoration' of Jews to the country in 1656, because the numbers involved over four and a half centuries run into millions. Beyond that, the primary records and sources for an examination of Scottish Jewry were available. The Scottish Jewish Archives Centre in Glasgow houses extensive collections of documents and other materials essential to this study. More critical from the perspective of a genealogical study, almost all the vital records (births, marriages and deaths) were accessible online for the period under review. In addition, national censuses of Scotland of a modern form were conducted every ten years from 1841 on (that is, just 25 years after the inception of Scottish Jewry) – and, more importantly, the censuses from 1841 to 1911 are now in the public domain and accessible online.

The project was framed as a demographic and genealogical survey of Scottish Jewry, whose goal was to address various aspects of Scottish Jewry as an immigrant community, which had not been scientifically researched thus far. These included:

▶ Identifying the vast majority of "Scottish Jews" (as defined by the project);

▶ Establishing the provenance of the Jewish immigrants (where they came from – mainly Central and Eastern Europe);

▶ Tracing their numbers over time;

▶ Analysing birth, marriage and death rates;

▶ Mapping the dispersal patterns of the Jewish immigrants throughout Scotland;

▶ Plotting residential shifts within Glasgow and, to a lesser extent, Edinburgh, reflecting socio-economic changes in the two major concentrations of Scottish Jewry;

▶ Producing occupational analyses;

▶ Identifying various élites (religious, business, cultural, political, etc.);

▶ Tracking the considerable body of trans-migrant Jews who passed through Scotland on their way to the United States and other destinations.

This clearly was to be a multidisciplinary study and we were fortunate in being able to assemble an extremely talented and distinguished team of experts, mainly resident in Scotland or Scottish by origin. Besides myself (a historian and genealogist), they included Dr Kenneth Collins, the leading contemporary historian of Scottish Jewry (Glasgow and Jerusalem); Prof Aubrey Newman, a social historian with a deep interest in Scottish Jewry (Leicester), Prof Gillian Raab, an applied statistician (Edinburgh); Prof Jack Ukeles, a demographer (Jerusalem) and Mr Harvey Kaplan, the Director of the Scottish Jewish Archives Centre (Glasgow). Our greatest good fortune was being able to enlist Mr Michael Tobias, a trained genealogist with extraordinary Information Technology skills (Glasgow).

To obtain his MSc in genealogy at the University of Strathclyde, Michael had written a thesis entitled "A Study of 19th Century Scottish Jewry". He very generously agreed to have his study incorporated into the IIJG project and built upon. The project found the ready sponsorship of the Glasgow Jewish Representative Council and of the Scottish Council of Jewish Communities. It also was accorded generous funding by a number of public and private charitable trusts, including the Heritage Lottery Fund (Scotland). Without their support, the project could not have been undertaken. We are immensely grateful.

The project is nearing completion and this book, written by Dr Collins, is its first tangible product. In advance of a scholarly monograph (to be published in 2017), it seeks to present the initial results of the research and to illustrate them through thumb-nail portraits of many of the men and women behind the dry numbers and statistics. Above all, it shows that much of the conventional wisdom about Scottish Jewry and its evolution needs to be revisited and revised, perhaps radically.

Dr Neville Lamdan
January, 2016
IIJG Chairman and Project Director, Jerusalem

Introduction

Imagine a history book where the author has access only to documents, learned articles, newspaper cuttings and books written by earlier researchers and perhaps some oral history reminiscences. Now consider this work, where the narrative history is informed not just by the studies which have gone before but by genealogical and demographic research using the latest techniques that technology has to offer. This innovative combination has produced the short account of Jewish life in Scotland you have before you, which is framed by accurate data, extending the searches to every area of Scotland, and gives an insight into topics previously unavailable to the historian. In many cases the data has served to confirm the published histories of Scotland's Jews and that confirmation is in itself of value, but it has added a special dimension by supplying, as we shall see, information that standard historical techniques cannot provide.

However, it should be clearly understood that this is not the history of Scotland's Jews but rather a history whose narrative follows the trends illustrated by the two recent studies. Consequently, it focusses on issues relating to themes generated in the study and important topics not dealt with, such as the organisational structure of the community, aspects of its philanthropy, the Zionist movement and the community during war-time, can be found in more detailed works as indicated in the Bibliography. Nevertheless, this book illuminates the growth and development of a Scottish minority community in a way which provides lessons for its integration into its new society.

It has been a happy combination of talents which has given me the possibility to provide this new account of the Jews in Scotland. This is, of necessity, an overview but one which will give future scholars and researchers some of the detail they will need to provide the context for their work. It was Dr Neville Lamdan, then Director of the International Institute for Jewish

Genealogy at the National Library of Israel in Jerusalem, who conceived the idea of a comprehensive demographic and genealogical study of the Jews in Scotland. His plans could not have come to fruition without the genealogical skills of Michael Tobias, Glasgow-based but with an international reputation for his ability to identify and retrieve data to produce the most comprehensive information possible. Without these two individuals the studies, in which this extensive exercise was conducted, would not have been possible.

We could not have predicted the complexity of what we were proposing at the outset. Michael Tobias trawled through almost a million online records, not to mention combing through digitalised newspaper reports and court records dating back to the eighteenth century. Once the data had been collected we were able to draw on the expertise of Professor Gillian Raab, an applied statistician whose fields of application are chiefly in medical and social statistics.

The task was not simple. Some individuals and families cannot be found online in the Census databases. There were some genuinely missed residents, sub-standard enumerators, missing schedules, poor quality schedules as well as badly transcribed data entry. The condition of many of the early records made legibility difficult at times. It also appears that sometimes people deliberately provided incorrect information. A pragmatic approach to identifying Jews was followed, principally using Jewish names, places of origin and community affiliation. Conversely, those with remote Jewish roots fell outwith the scope of this study. Jewish transmigrants, who were only briefly in the country, could only be included if they were in Scotland long enough to be included in an official document, such as a Census.

Although most of the information could be accessed electronically there are many pitfalls in trying to identify Jews solely on the basis of names or even place of origin. Many of the earliest German-Jewish immigrants did not use identifiably Jewish first names or surnames and in many cases they were heavily assimilated even before leaving Germany. However, where some evidence of their Jewishness has been identified, possibly through attachment to a synagogue or burial in a Jewish cemetery, those families have been included in this work. There was also a significant migration of Lithuanian Catholics to Scotland, around the end of the nineteenth century, mostly to work in the Lanarkshire coal mines. However, their names, occupation and geographical concentration made them distinctive and so they could be excluded from our study.

As Jews settled in Scotland and began to adapt to their surroundings many began to anglicise their surnames. Others changed their names for reasons connected with work; many doctors, for example found, as late as the 1940s, that a distinctively Jewish surname was a bar to employment. According to Jewish Law a Jew is the child of a Jewish mother who has either been born Jewish or has been converted to Judaism. The study has followed Jews as they have arrived in Scotland, migrated round the country and settled in various locations. We have followed them through several generations using all the data available but where people have married out of the religion and the next generation has shown no links with the Jewish community, or indeed any form of Jewish life or attachment, we have accepted that they cease to be part of the Jewish story in Scotland. Some of the stories in the book illustrate aspects of that process.

The cost of obtaining the information in this study proved to be more than could have been predicted. Accessing such a vast array of records was also an expensive exercise as we were given no special assistance, considering the number of files consulted, by National Records of Scotland, formed in 2011 following a merger between the General Register Office for Scotland (GROS) and the National Archives of Scotland. The project Scotland's Jews: Profiling the immigrant Experience was substantially funded by the Heritage Lottery Foundation (OH13-21040) and built on an earlier study, Two Centuries of Scottish Jewry - A Demographic and Genealogical Profile. These projects were also supported by a number of Jewish trusts and benefactors with Scottish connections and their contribution is gratefully recognised in the book's Acknowledgements.

This book will also show that just as Scotland has enriched the life of its Jews so have Scottish Jews enriched the life of Scotland. We shall see, for example, how Benno Schotz, Josef Herman and Jankel Adler contributed to Scottish art while Karl Abenheimer and Joseph Schorstein contributed to Scottish philosophy and Avrom Greenbaum added an extra dimension to community drama. Further examples from the legal and medical professions will confirm the legacy of the great wave of migration from Eastern Europe that brought thousands of Jews to Scotland.

The book indicates sources for further study in the Bibliography, rather than provide the references usually associated with more academic works, and will show what information has been identified from the special research carried out for the two projects. The existence of the Scottish Jewish Archives Centre has spurred widespread interest in the Jewish story in Scotland and numerous books, pamphlets, articles, family and personal testimonies and videos as well as academic theses and dissertations have appeared in recent decades. This has ensured that many aspects of the Scottish narrative now indicate the Jewish role in many walks of Scottish life. We trust that this book will provide more insight into that narrative.

Dr Kenneth Collins

Acknowledgements

This book draws the basis for its information from two major research projects: Two Centuries of Scottish Jewry – A Demographic and Genealogical Profile and Scotland's Jews: Profiling the Immigrant Experience. The latter study was substantially funded by the Heritage Lottery Fund and a number of Jewish charitable trusts also provided valued support. We would like to acknowledge the financial support of: the International Institute for Jewish Genealogy, the Glasgow Jewish Community Trust, Glasgow Jewish Representative Council, Netherlee and Clarkston Synagogue Charitable Trust, Queens Park Synagogue Charitable Trust as well as John Dover and the Esterson Trust, Malcolm Livingstone and David Cohen. We are also grateful to Michael Tobias for applying his grant funding to the cost of data retrieval.

SCoJeC, the Glasgow Jewish Representative Council and the Scottish Jewish Archives Centre have provided practical support and after the final completion of all aspects of the second study the Archives Centre will host the collected data.

A number of individuals, both in Scotland and in Israel, have provided valuable advice and some have been involved in aspects of research. Prof Gillian Raab provided statistical analyses of much of the research data that had been compiled by Michael Tobias. Harvey Kaplan has assisted during the study in extracting census data, identifying existing source material already in the Archives Centre collections and has been of considerable assistance in providing information as it has been required during the writing of this book as well as identifying appropriate illustrations from the collections of the Scottish Jewish Archives Centre. The advice of Aubrey Newman and Nicholas Evans has been freely given and has been much appreciated. I am indebted to Professor Elliot Berry of the Hebrew University of Jerusalem for sharing the memoirs of his grandfather with me. Excerpts of this document, which is an authentic account of migrating to Glasgow and working conditions in the city in the first decade of the twentieth century, forms Chapter 5 of this book. Finally, my thanks to Dianna Wolfson and Harvey Kaplan for their meticulous proof-reading and attention to detail.

1739 Jacob de Castro Sarmento, London-based refugee from the Portuguese Inquisition, awarded MD degree at Marischal College, Aberdeen the first medical degree awarded to a Jew in the English speaking world.

1779 Joseph Hart Myers from London graduated at the University of Edinburgh.

1802 Heyman Lion, Edinburgh dentist and chiropodist, published his book on *Spinae Pedum* (Corns).

1803 Abraham Hayman and Israel Lob Reiss arrived in Glasgow where they lived and traded for some years.

1816/1817 Edinburgh Hebrew Congregation opened the first synagogue in Scotland.

1819 First Jewish cemetery at Braid Place, Edinburgh.

1821 Glasgow Hebrew Congregation opened a small synagogue in the High Street.

1822 Scotland's first Jewish marriage, in Edinburgh, reported in the *Glasgow Herald*.

1831 First Jewish cemetery in Glasgow opened as part of the new Glasgow Necropolis.

1838 Edinburgh Jewish Communal Philanthropic Society established.

1839 Louis Ashenheim (Edinburgh) graduated in Medicine, the first Scottish born Jew to do so.

1842 Glasgow Synagogue moved to 204 George Street. Its location at the Andersonian University Anatomy building provoked a schism.

1855 First burial in Jewish section of Glasgow's Janefield Cemetery (Eastern Necropolis.)

1858 Glasgow Synagogue moved to larger premises at corner of George Street and John Street.

1858 Glasgow Hebrew Philanthropic Society founded.

1878 Dundee Synagogue established.

1879 Garnethill Synagogue opened – the first purpose-built synagogue in Scotland.

1880 First synagogue opened south of the Clyde in Commerce Street.

1880 Kosher butcher shop opened in the Gorbals.

1882 *RUSSIA'S ANTI-SEMITIC MAY LAWS PROVOKES MAJOR JEWISH WESTWARD MIGRATION.*

1883 Communal leader Michael Simons elected to Glasgow Corporation later appointed a Bailie.

1888 Glasgow Hebrew Benevolent Loan Society founded.

1888 Edinburgh Jewish Literary Society founded.

1890s Jewish communities established in Aberdeen and Greenock.

1890 Glasgow Jewish Board of Guardians formed from the Hebrew Philanthropic Society.

1890 Chovevei Zion – first Zionist society in Scotland founded in Edinburgh. Glasgow's branch opens one year later.

1891 *JEWS EXCLUDED FROM MANY RUSSIAN TOWNS AND CITIES, LEADING TO FURTHER JEWISH MIGRATION.*

1892 Main Street Synagogue opened – the first major Gorbals synagogue.

1895 Glasgow Talmud Torah founded, providing Jewish education after school hours and on Sundays.

1896 Graham Street Synagogue, Edinburgh, opened.

1897 Glasgow Jewish Strangers Aid Society opened a hostel for transmigrants.

1898-1906 Glasgow United Synagogue linked all the city's synagogues.

1900s Communities formed in Ayr, Falkirk, Inverness and Dunfermline.

1901 Great Synagogue opened in South Portland Street. When it closed in 1974, it was the last Jewish building in the Gorbals.

1903 & 1905 *POGROMS IN KISHINEV LEFT DOZENS OF JEWS KILLED AND HOMES AND BUSINESSES DESTROYED.*

1905 *ALIENS ACT PLACED RESTRICTIONS ON FOREIGN IMMIGRATION.*

1906 Queens Park Synagogue founded: the first Glasgow synagogue south of the Gorbals.

1908 Glasgow Yeshiva (Rabbinical College) founded.

1909 Jewish Students' Society founded at Edinburgh University. A Jewish Students' Society at Glasgow University was founded in 1911.

1912 Glasgow Beth Din (Court of Jewish Religious Law) founded.

1914 Glasgow Jewish Representative Council founded: the oldest Jewish representative body in Britain outside London.

1914-1918 *FIRST WORLD WAR CAUSED MAJOR DISRUPTION TO JEWISH COMMUNITIES IN EASTERN EUROPE.*

1918 Rabbi Salis Daiches appointed rabbi in Edinburgh.

1927 Oscar Slater released from jail after 20 years imprisonment for a murder he did not commit.

1928 *Jewish Echo*, Scotland's first English-language Jewish newspaper began publication.

1931 Glasgow Progressive Synagogue established.

1932 Opening of new Edinburgh Synagogue in Salisbury Road.

1933 *NAZI POWER IN GERMANY UNLEASHED ANTI-SEMITIC MEASURES WHICH EVENTUALLY LEADS TO THE HOLOCAUST.*

1933-1939 Nazi anti-Semitism leads to arrival of Jewish refugees in Scotland.

1934 Giffnock and Newlands Synagogue opened. In its present building it is the largest synagogue in Scotland.

1938 *FOLLOWING NAZI POGROM, KRISTALLNACHT, IN NOVEMBER BRITAIN AGREED TO ADMIT 10,000 JEWISH CHILDREN (KINDERTRANSPORT.)*

1948 *STATE OF ISRAEL ESTABLISHED.*

1950

1951 *GLASGOW FESTIVAL OF JEWISH CULTURE AS PART OF THE FESTIVAL OF BRITAIN. A FURTHER AMBITIOUS JEWISH FESTIVAL WAS HELD IN 1990 DURING GLASGOW'S YEAR AS EUROPEAN CITY OF CULTURE.*

1962 Calderwood Lodge Jewish Primary School opened, the only Jewish school in Scotland. Became a state school in 1982.

1963 Benno Schotz appointed Queens' Sculptor in Ordinary for Scotland.

1969 Glasgow Maccabi took over former Giffnock Synagogue building as sports and leisure centre. The site eventually also became the base for Jewish welfare agencies.

1973 Following Dundee slum clearance the City Council provided a new building for the Dundee Hebrew Congregation.

1980 Reconstruction of Edinburgh Synagogue to produce smaller synagogue with a community centre on the premises.

1986 Malcolm Rifkind became the first Jew in Scotland to hold Cabinet office on his appointment as Secretary of State for Scotland.

1987 Scottish Jewish Archives Centre founded to collect, preserve and display Scotland's Jewish heritage.

1996 Glasgow Jewish Welfare Board (previously the Glasgow Jewish Board of Guardians) professionalised and became Jewish Care Scotland.

1999 *SCOTTISH PARLIAMENT ESTABLISHED.*

1999 Scottish Council of Jewish Communities formed replacing the Scottish Jewish Standing Committee established in 1983.

2000

Establishing Community

1816–1817

Jacob de Castro Sarmento MD
Marischal College,
Aberdeen.
*The first Jewish medical
graduate in the English
speaking world, 1739.*

It is never easy to know where to begin the story of the Jews in Scotland but it certainly starts before the first Census in 1801. We know that individual Jews have lived, worked and traded in the country from the time that David Pardo (or Brown) was accepted as a trader in Edinburgh at the end of the seventeenth century. An unnamed Jew, in Glasgow, was recorded as being awarded 'ten dollors' by a Burgh Court as far back as March 1662. Converted Jews appear at the universities from the seventeenth century. Julius Conradus Otto, possibly identified with Naphtali Margolioth of Vienna, who occupied the Chair of Hebrew and Oriental Languages at Edinburgh University from 1642, was one of these, although it is recorded that he later returned to Judaism. Jewish names appear on the graduate rolls of Aberdeen University from 1739 and we can speculate on Jewish activity in earlier centuries. Jewish financiers, probably based in England, before the expulsion of Jews from there in 1290, have been recorded as providing loans for an impoverished Scottish court and even supporting church properties around both Glasgow and Edinburgh.

However, it is customary to begin the story with an organised community, where a group of Jews who are settled in a compact locality come together for prayer, kosher food and support for the poor. We now consider that the previously accepted dates for this development – 1816 in Edinburgh and 1823 in Glasgow - should probably be revised to 1817 and 1821 respectively. Indeed, we have been able to identify Jews in the Scottish cities a few years before forming a community in all but name, and in the case of Edinburgh some decades before formal communities were established.

The population of Scotland was fairly homogeneous at the end of the eighteenth century. The major migrations from Ireland, but also from Italy and of course the Jewish arrivals from Central and Eastern Europe, still lay many decades into the future. Jews, also, were afraid to have too much of a public profile, preferring to keep much to themselves, and thus avoiding the slights of an anti-Semitism they had encountered previously in their countries of origin. It took some courage, therefore, for the formal establishment of a Jewish community as an indicator that the Jewish residents of a particular Scottish city or town were there permanently. When the first more substantial synagogue was consecrated in 1858, in Glasgow's George Street, a Christian observer remarked that the event actually caused him pain, writing in the *Glasgow Herald* of 7th September 1858 that:

> *'The sight of so many Jews assembled, and the Laws of Moses, partially observed, were novel and interesting. The appearance of so many (Jews) setting aside the best evidence of the most blessed (Christian) testimony is humbling and distressing'.*

During the 1780s we have definite evidence of Jewish settlement in Edinburgh. Besides the presence of Jewish medical students at the University, attracted by the absence of religious tests required for university students in England, there were a number of disparate individuals who made up the first groupings of Jewish Scots. Prominent among these was Herman (or Heyman) Lion (1748-1825) and his wife. Lion was a colourful and flamboyant character who had hailed from Germany and was practising in Edinburgh both as a dentist and a chiropodist, then described as a 'corn operator', but also making forays to Glasgow to deal with some clients there. Lion produced a remarkable book on treating corns, stretching to over four hundred pages and, at some stage, he decided that if he knew so much about care of the feet he ought to attend classes at the university and qualify as a physician.

This proved to be an ultimately unrewarding experience. He enrolled and took classes between 1790 and 1795, but the Edinburgh University Senate refused to give him a degree without supplying any reason. He then took himself off to King's College, Aberdeen, where MD degrees were awarded on the basis of affidavits from physicians in good standing, and which he had obtained. He was again turned down, not because he did not have the quali-fications for the degree but on account 'of the line of practice (chiropody) which he has for some time adopted'. We have no reason to believe that his medical qualification was rejected in both Edinburgh and Aberdeen for any reason other than medical snobbery.

Lion ensured an enduring legacy for himself and his wife by the purchase of a burial plot from the City Council, for seventeen pounds sterling, in May 1795 on Calton Hill, a geographical position of great prominence in the heart of Edinburgh. This small burial ground was indicated on the 1852 Ordnance Survey map as 'Jews' Burial Vault', situated close to the Royal Observatory.

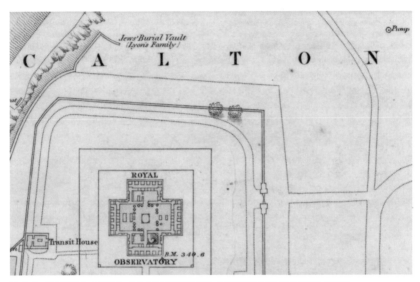

Detail of Ordinance Survey Map of Calton Hill, Edinburgh showing the Royal Observatory and the Burial Vault for Herman Lion and his wife (1852).

This was Edinburgh's only Jewish cemetery until the provision of a regular Jewish burial ground which quickly followed the establishment of the synagogue, situated in Braid Place and opening in 1819. Lion's descendants, through his daughters, Sophie and Fanny, include many surgeon-dentists in the Eskell and de Saxe families to be found all over the world, including Albert Eskells, and family, who was in Glasgow during the 1860s.

More successful Jewish medical students of the period in Edinburgh included Joseph Hart Myers, from New York, whose MD degree in 1779 was the first awarded to a Jew in Britain after a due period of undergraduate study, Solomon de Leon from the island of St Kitts in the West Indies and Levi Myers from South Carolina. However, it is the colourful and disputatious group of artisans who formed the core of the first Jewish community in Scotland and this was certainly in place during the 1780s. Abraham Barnet, later known as

Francis Burlin, arrived in Edinburgh around 1777 and, in various legal documents related to a libel case in which he was involved, he described himself as being the longest residing Jew in Edinburgh and as the leader of the Jews in the city. Burlin, listed as a drawing master, despite being the leader of the community was in fact married to a non-Jewish woman called Alison Chamber. Burlin was responsible for arranging for another Jewish resident, Henry Daniel, to be able to go to London to be trained as a *shochet*, to provide kosher meat, or at least poultry for Edinburgh's Jews. Francis Burlin was taken to court in a libel case by Rose Nathan, described as 'the only Jewish woman in Edinburgh', and her husband, the same Henry Daniel, after Burlin had accused Rose of sexual impropriety, by committing adultery with her then lodger Heyman Lion.

Identification of foreign residents becomes easier with the requirements for the registration of aliens in 1794, when it could be noted that most Jews in the city hailed from Germany or Holland. One such newcomer, Moses Daniel, a spectacle maker from Hanover, signed his name in Hebrew characters, on 28 July 1798. He had been living in Edinburgh's Canongate for 13 years having entered Britain at Gravesend from Holland in 1775.

In a detailed account of Levi Myer's experiences in Edinburgh, there is little reference to the social life he enjoyed in the city, so we know nothing of his involvement either with the student medical societies or with Burlin's Jewish group. However, during the last decade of the eighteenth century and the first decade of the nineteenth century the local community became accustomed to the various Jewish visitors to Scotland. These included William Brodum and Samuel Solomon, producers of popular but unregulated medication, Daniel Mendoza, the boxer, and the Danish dentist Philip Aron, who was in Scotland around 1801 before moving on to Ireland.

Dr Levi Myers MD (Glasgow) 1765–1827, from South Carolina, studied at the University of Edinburgh from 1785 to 1787.

A young Jewish merchant, Israel Lob Reiss, arrived in Glasgow from Germany in 1803, but soon ran into problems with orders and payments and seems to have left the city after living and trading there for four years. Around the same time Abraham Hayman (1773-1823), a Jewish silk merchant and dealer settled in Glasgow. In 1806 he married Janet Hamilton, a non-Jewish widow, and sometime after her death in 1815 he moved to Edinburgh.

The Beginnings of Community

This phenomenon of waiting until the local Jews were confident enough to announce the formal structure of a Hebrew Congregation can be identified in Glasgow and Aberdeen also. Census figures indicate that Jewish communities, in general, came to be established in the various centres in Scotland once the Jewish population exceeded thirty members. Thus, communities were established in Falkirk and Dunfermline in the first decade of the twentieth century, when there were more than thirty Jewish residents in each of the two towns. A community was established in Greenock in 1894 by which time there had already been almost 40 Jewish births beginning in the 1870s. Jews in Inverness managed to form and maintain their community, with synagogue, minister/*shochet* and cemetery around the same time, with barely twenty Jews. However, their own reports of their activities, sent to the *Jewish Chronicle* in London, suggest a somewhat larger group than indicated in the 1901 Census with around twenty families by 1906. There were more than thirty Jews in Aberdeen as early as 1871 and when the community was established some twenty years later, in 1893, the numbers had hardly changed at all. It was noted that the leading figures in the new community, such as its chairman Alexander Zamek, had been in Aberdeen for many years and it had taken some time for them to feel confident enough to make their community known to the wider public.

We consider that the Glasgow Hebrew Congregation, with its synagogue in a small apartment at 43 High Street, was established in 1821. In May of 1821 Sir Moses and Lady Montefiore had visited Glasgow, as part of a tour of Scotland, and they paid a call on Moses Lisenheim, the community's first minister and *shochet*. Fears of making a public announcement of an established presence were fuelled by a fear of local prejudices. One contemporary example is the statement made by John Cleland, in his book *The Rise and Progress of the City of Glasgow* published in 1820:

> '... that particular part of the Saltmarket Street, may be said to be the Jews' corner of Glasgow. In it – all that is dissolute and wretched is to be found; in it – the most worthless of both sexes assemble on the Lord's day for the worst of purposes.'

We have some interesting details of the new community in Glasgow, because of the details recorded in the 1831 Census, showing that only five members of the community had been born in Glasgow. Some hailed from Poland (11), Germany (12) and Holland (3) and a further five had been born in London and ten more in the small Kent town of Sheerness. A Jewish community had grown up in the Chatham area of Kent providing services for the Royal Navy and an offshoot of this community established itself in Sheerness around 1790. Members of the community appear to have been linked to various crimes, serious enough to warrant one to be sentenced to transportation to Australia and one Jew was actually executed for his part in a robbery. By the 1830s the small Sheerness community was already in decline, no doubt hastened by the movement of ten of its members to Glasgow. Jonas Michael and family left Sheerness for Glasgow operating a furniture warehouse in Candleriggs by 1822. His son, Michael, was one of Glasgow's first *shochtim*. Although the nucleus of a Jewish community in Glasgow dates back several years before 1821 it was not until 1831 that the community obtained its first burial ground, at the prestigious Glasgow Necropolis, laid out in the style of the Père la Chaise cemetery in Paris, purchasing space for around fifty internments for the sum of 100 guineas. There is no indication of where previous Jewish burials in Glasgow had taken place, though there are suggestions that Glasgow's Jewish dead were being buried in Edinburgh, as it is extremely unlikely that there had been no deaths in the community for more than a decade.

One of the most bizarre episodes at that time concerned the Schwabe family, who decided in 1860, some years in advance of their move out of Glasgow to remove their children's bodies clandestinely from the Jewish cemetery at the Glasgow Necropolis and re-inter them in a Christian burial ground. No satisfactory answer has been provided for this strange act other than perhaps to remove any trace of their Jewish origins, a move that clearly failed as the story still resonates a century and a half later.

The Entrance Arch and Obelisk at the Jews' Enclosure of the Glasgow Necropolis (1832). The illustration shows the area after the completion of restoration in 2015. The new ornamental gate has the original gateposts with quotations from the Biblical Book of Lamentations and from Lord Byron's Hebrew melodies.

Census records indicate that these early communities took many years to consolidate. Even as the number of Jews in Scotland grew substantially during the nineteenth century there was a not a single decade where a majority of Jews identified in a Census were still in the same town or city ten years later. Even in 1891, when the number of Jews in Glasgow was more than three thousand, slightly less than half could be identified there in the 1901 Census. By the middle of the nineteenth century the Census figures reveal that almost half of the Jews living in Scotland had been born there, a proportion which fell to around a third by the end of the nineteenth century as the level of immigration increased.

The Censuses also reveal a spread of Jews around the country and not just in the main cities and towns. While three quarters of Scottish Jews were in Glasgow in 1901, and just under a fifth in Edinburgh, there were a few Jews in the Orkney Isles in 1871, seventeen Jews in Moray in 1901 and fifteen Jews in Perthshire in 1871, but only ten some thirty years later.

We shall examine this phenomenon of community growth and contraction in more detail as we continue to review the facts of dispersal of Scotland's Jews and its implications as they spread around the country virtually from the time of their arrival.

Consolidation
of Community

1816–1880

With the establishment of small Jewish communities in Edinburgh and Glasgow in the first decades of the nineteenth century, the scene was set for the slow growth which followed over the next decades. While individual Jews could be found in various locations around Scotland, almost all were based in these two communities until the arrival of a number of Jews from Germany in Dundee and the establishment of a community there in 1878. We can plot the growth of the communities in Glasgow and Edinburgh through the nineteenth century with the help of Census data.

The few dozen Jews in Glasgow at the beginning of the established community had grown to just over a hundred in 1841. Numbers were around two hundred when the first major synagogue was opened in George Street in 1858. In the survey of regional communities in 1846, produced for Chief Rabbi Nathan Adler, Glasgow's hundred Jews had two synagogues. This followed a personal dispute which led to the formation of a 'New Synagogue', which was located in the building of the Anatomy Department of Anderson's University, and considered by the 'Old Synagogue' members to be an 'unfit place for worship'.

Contemporary records indicate some debate about the number of Jews in the city as the ambitious plans for conversion of the building, located near George Square, advanced. With a *mikva*, classrooms as well as a synagogue, with seats for two hundred men and sixty women, the plans indicated a more settled community that had outgrown the small rooms in different apartments which had previously served as the community bases.

The community at this stage had a number of more assimilated German Jews, who had been sent to Scotland by Hamburg-based Jewish-owned textile firms as their agents and who usually attended the synagogue only on the High Holy Days. Given the size of community, as identified in the Censuses in 1851 and 1861 it would seem that the synagogue leaders were justified in their plans for the new synagogue and they could safely ignore claims that there were just a couple of dozen Jewish families in the city. The opening of the new synagogue also gave evidence of a new attempt at community unity given the various schisms and squabbles which had occurred in the past with two tiny synagogues operating in desperate competition. However, such divisions were not over and a further breakaway group was formed in 1870. By this time the Census indicates that there were around 400 Jews in Glasgow and not the forty families claimed by the main community body trying to persuade the Chief Rabbi that there was only room for one synagogue in the city!

Around this time the Glasgow Hebrew Congregation devised a rule to keep control of the growing community in the hands of its more senior, and more affluent, members. Accordingly, a two-tier scheme was instituted whereby regular worshippers would be seat-holders but decision-making would be in the hands of the synagogue membership, a status only available by election, and at an extra fee, voted on only by existing members. The members of the Congregation were the various city merchants who had become prosperous during their residence in Glasgow having established successful businesses.

Beginnings of Jewish Gorbals

However, by the time of the 1871 Census there were already around eighty Jews living south of the River Clyde in the Gorbals and the adjacent districts of Tradeston and Hutchesontown. Ten years later this number had grown to over four hundred. The days when the Jewish community of Glasgow could be organised in just one synagogue were clearly over. I pointed out in *Second City Jewry* that the choice of a site at Garnethill for the new Glasgow synagogue was not universally popular given the number of poorer Jews living in the Saltmarket area just north of the Clyde, along with the Jews in the Gorbals to the south. As a concession, rooms were made available in Stockwell Street for Hebrew classes and Shabbat prayers during the winter of 1879, just after the new synagogue at Garnethill opened. This clearly did not satisfy the residents of the Gorbals who found the Shabbat walk to Garnethill unacceptable and it was not surprising that 1880 saw the opening of small prayer rooms in Commerce Street, in Tradeston at the edge of the Gorbals. Further synagogues south of the river followed.

Occupation details listed in the Censuses show that the early community members were substantially involved in merchant trading and the growth of the so-called ghetto trades, primarily in the manufacture of clothing but later also furniture and picture frames, only became significant as the communities grew significantly in the last two decades of the nineteenth century. The Levenstons, who had a number of musicians in the family besides those involved in medical botany, made their mark in Glasgow. Michael Jacob

Levenston had been born in London in 1799 and moved first to Edinburgh before settling in Glasgow around 1850 with his three grown up sons William, Solomon Alexander and Samuel, as well as some younger children. Michael Jacob and his older sons began in business as herbalists describing themselves as 'doctors of medicine' a designation to which they were certainly not entitled. Samuel, a synagogue trustee in 1858 and again in 1879, decided to study at Glasgow University and actually qualified as a doctor becoming the only university graduate in the community. However, the lure of the family business proved too strong and he was struck off the Medical Register for unprofessional activities related to the sale of medications and the production of pamphlets alleged to be of a scurrilous nature. The Levenstons had premises around the Glasgow city centre and were also active in Aberdeen and Greenock as well as other places around Scotland.

LIFE BALSAM,
Established 33 years, in Glasgow.

NEW REMEDY.—This recently discovered Medicine thoroughly invigorates the Brain, Nerves, and Muscles, re-energises the failing Functions of Life, and rapidly Cures every form of Nervous Debility, Indigestion, Depression, Loss of Power, Nervous and Mind Diseases, from whatever causes. Sold by the Proprietor in cases, Price 11s, and 33s. Sent to any Address, Steamboat or Coach Office, or Railway Station till called for, on receipt of P.O.O. for amount, made payable to Joseph Levenston, the Money Order Office, Glasgow. Descriptive Pamphlet sent on request. 2 Stamps.
All letters must be addressed JOSEPH LEVENSTON, Esq,. 46, Oxford Street, S.S., Glasgow.

Advertisements such as these by Jewish traders or charlatans, rather than physicians, illustrate a popular desire for a variety of medicines.

The Levenstons clearly had come to Glasgow from England because of what the developing middle classes offered to the newcomers in terms of acceptance and integration. Benjamin Simons also left London looking for business opportunities. He passed through Newcastle and Edinburgh before deciding to start a fruit broking company in Glasgow in 1849 which he developed into the largest fruit brokerage in the world, with branches in London and New York. His son, Michael, achieved prominence as a city councillor and patron of the arts while active in the Jewish community, of which he was for many years its undisputed leader. Michael, a city bailie, was also a founder of the Howard and Wyndham Theatre Company with another prominent member of the Garnethill Synagogue, David Heilbron, a whisky merchant and distiller. The Simons family chaired Howard and Wyndham for fifty years, and expanded it to twenty-five theatres outside London.

Community growth in Edinburgh matched that in Glasgow until the middle of the nineteenth century but from then on there were far more Jews settling in Glasgow. As Glasgow was a great port city, with regular steamer departures for New York, as well as a major commercial and industrial centre, there were more economic opportunities for Jews settling in the city. Because of the easy access to North America, starting a new life there was always possible if and when they were ready to move on. The number of Jews in Edinburgh hardly changed in the twenty years between 1851 and 1871 and despite a spurt in growth during the 1880s, not matched in Glasgow, the concentration of Jewish life in Scotland remained in the west. In addition, fewer Jews were passing through Leith and Edinburgh on the transmigrant route, in the years before the First World War as the number of steamers bringing migrants to Leith had dropped substantially. Most travellers were now reaching Glasgow by train from Hull or Grimsby, rather than from Edinburgh. Estimates by the Glasgow Corporation Sanitation Department that the number of Jews passing through Glasgow around 1910 was increasing and formed the majority of emigrants from Russia have not been borne out by analysis of figures for Jews arriving in New York.

The First Synagogues and Ministers in Edinburgh

The early history of the Edinburgh Hebrew Congregation is closely associated with its long-serving minister Rev Moses Joel (1788-1863) who came to Edinburgh from Bavaria around 1818 but may not have served as its religious leader till around 1828 when Meir Rintel had left town. The earliest surviving Jewish document in Scotland, a copy of which is now

Rev Moses Joel, (1788-1863) early minister to the Edinburgh Hebrew Congregation for over 30 years. (Illustration courtesy of Edinburgh Libraries)

held at the Scottish Jewish Archives Centre, is Joel's register of circumcisions, carried out between December 1830 and June 1860, and containing 95 names. It seems likely therefore that Rintel, described as a 'scholarly contro-versialist' by Cecil Roth, was Joel's predecessor, though he had only arrived in town around after 1818, by which time the community had already been established. Rintel, was the friend of Chief Rabbi Solomon Hirschell and author of a number of Hebrew works.

The first Edinburgh synagogue was situated in Richmond Court remaining there until it moved to Park Place in 1868. Lest it be thought that Edinburgh Jews were less schismatic than their co-religionists in Glasgow or Dundee in these early days, it is worth noting that some historians have suggested that there were two synagogues operating in Richmond Court between 1833 and 1840. However, a careful reading of the records indicates, that while tensions may have existed between different immigrant groups, there was only one synagogue in the city at the time.

This map of Robert Kirkwood (1817) shows the area around Nicolson Street and North Richmond Street where the early prayer houses and synagogues of the Edinburgh Hebrew Congregation were situated.
(Reproduced by permission of the Trustees of the National Library of Scotland).

However, as the Edinburgh community grew during the nineteenth century several small synagogues did develop. Firstly, the major synagogue, which had previously been in Park Place moved to larger premises in

THE JEWISH EXPERIENCE IN SCOTLAND
2: CONSOLIDATION OF COMMUNITY   29

Census Year	Jews in Scotland	Scottish Born	Persis- tence	Jews in Glasgow	Jews in Edinburgh
1841	335	44%	32%	130	152
1851	362	40%	33%	192	126
1861	444	45%	33%	227	156
1871	835	41%	35%	440	244
1881	1651	41%	46%	1057	356
1891	3254	37%	53%	1945	993
1901	9079	35%	43%	6862	1629
1911	11753	42%		8918	2042

This Table illustrates Jewish Community Growth during the 19th Century. Persistence indicates the percentage of the community in the previous Census still present at the next one, showing that Scotland was a staging post on the route to North America. From 1911 population growth was largely through natural increase rather than inward migration. (Courtesy Michael Tobias)

Elizabeth (Betsy) Isaacs (née Levenston) was born in Edinburgh in 1832 when there were barely a hundred Jews in the city. She lived all her adult life in Edinburgh and when she joined her children in London, not long before her death in 1912, the Edinburgh community had grown to over two thousand.

Graham Street in 1896. At the same time the Edinburgh New Hebrew Congregation, in Richmond Court, reflected the customs of the most recent, and more religious, arrivals. The synagogue in Graham Street had what was described as a more 'English' outlook, as befitted members who had been longer in the city, while the smaller places of worship represented the Yiddish speaking 'greeners'. One synagogue, the tin-roofed or *blechene* shul, a mile or two away belonged to the waterproofers of the Caledonian Rubber Company in the Dalry district while another was more Chassidic in outlook.

Outside Glasgow and Edinburgh it was only in Dundee and Aberdeen that Jews settled in any numbers before the beginnings of the major wave of immigration of the last decades of the nineteenth century. There were less than a dozen Jews in Dundee in 1861 but a decade later there were forty, a figure which we have noted elsewhere was sufficient to establish a community. By 1881 this had grown to almost 70. Numbers were just a little less in Aberdeen though as we have seen it was 1893 before the Aberdeen Hebrew Congregation was founded while the Dundee community was established in 1878[1].

Jewish Agents of German Textile Companies Established in Dundee

There were commercial links between a Dundee merchant and some Jewish traders in Amsterdam as early as 1634 and Jewish agents of German textile companies, mainly based in Hamburg, began arriving in Dundee in small numbers from the 1840s, buying jute products, linens and other textiles. This gave the origins of the Dundee community a different geographical and religious orientation from those in the other cities and towns in Scotland. By 1850 around a dozen Jewish textile firms in Hamburg were represented in Dundee. While many of their agents eventually became independent traders in Dundee, it is possible that some Jewish agents were based in Glasgow or even travelled regularly from Germany. They were heavily involved in Dundee's extensive jute industry and were instrumental in developing markets for its products around the world. Many of the agents were not religiously observant and those who arrived in the earlier years, when there was no organised Jewish community, quickly assimilated into the regular life of the city. In general, this was a prosperous group which added much to the social and cultural life of Dundee.

However, it was one of the German agents, Julius Weinberg, who was instrumental in the establishment of the first synagogue in 1878 in co-operation with the newly arrived, much more traditional and Yiddish speaking newcomers. There were naturally tensions between these two groups, coming from such different backgrounds, and for a time there were

---

1   While the traditional date for the founding of the Dundee Hebrew Congregation is 1874 it would seem from contemporary sources that the first synagogue service in Dundee only took place in 1878.

two groups, representing the different traditions, though it was the Eastern European community which was to survive down to modern times. German Jewish merchants and agents set up a Reform Synagogue in Bradford in 1873 but the numbers in Dundee seem to have been too small for this to have been a viable option there. Interestingly, one of the Dundee Jewish firms, Samson and Unna, carried the same name as that of Jacob Unna, founder of the Bradford (Reform) Synagogue. Despite the small numbers this 'Russian' community too was the subject of a schism and for a time Dundee had two separate Orthodox synagogues, possibly reflecting the different geographical origins or perhaps class and occupational divisions, sometimes related to the length of time the newcomers had been settled in the town.

Community leaders generally believed that Jewish education was the key to survival as a minority society in their new country. Consequently, all the communities maintained their own Hebrew classes, the *cheder*, usually entrusted to the care of their ministers. As these men were usually recent immigrants themselves they were often perceived as providing a service which was unable to compete with the standard of schooling provided by the civic bodies. Dull and unimaginative teaching, for two or three hours after each long school day, except Friday, was often looked at, in retrospect, as one of the weakest aspects of Jewish childhood. Garnethill Synagogue insisted, from early in the twentieth century, on having native English speakers as teachers, usually medical students, but the *cheder* system provided was hard to change. A claim in the Glasgow Jewish Representative Council's *Yearbook* in 1938, that the task of providing a modern Jewish education system with English speaking teachers had been almost completed, was somewhat premature.

Attempts had been made from the first decades of the twentieth century to set up a Jewish school in Glasgow, strongly supported by the Glasgow Jewish Representative Council, but the Education Authority was unwilling to match the requirements of the Jewish community. An attempt to set up a Hebrew medium school before the First World War also proved to be unsuccessful. Only one Jewish day school, Calderwood Lodge in Glasgow, was ever established in Scotland, and that only in 1962. The school grew very quickly in its early years, supported by around two thirds of the Jewish school children in the community, with its heyday in the 1980s. Calderwood Lodge became a state school in January 1982 and is now administered by East Renfrewshire Council, the area which is home to the majority of Jewish children attending the school.

Eastern European Migration

1880–1914

A s we have seen, Jews had been arriving in small numbers in Scotland throughout the nineteenth century. Some had arrived directly from Eastern Europe but in the main Jews who had reached Scotland before large scale immigration began in the last quarter of the nineteenth century, had come from Germany and Holland or had travelled north from England. Growing poverty in the Russian Pale of Settlement where Jews were confined by law, huge population growth and state sanctioned anti-Semitism were the drivers of this exodus and Scotland was situated on one of the main migrant routes taking Scandinavians, Lithuanians and many others, besides Jews, to North America.

From Hamburg or Rotterdam, Jewish migrants could travel across Scotland, from Leith or Dundee, on to Glasgow to wait for their steamer to the New World. Alternatively, they could stay for a while, learn a new trade and pick up some English. Some remained but the majority moved on with some taking many months or even years to leave. While the restrictive and discriminatory May Laws helped to spur the mass movement of Jews westwards in 1882 the number of Jews in Scotland only began to grow rapidly a decade later as financial pressures, expulsions and pogroms, religiously motivated violence, increased.

The Scottish transmigrant route, taking passengers from Hamburg through Leith, ran in substantial numbers from 1881 until a near shutdown in traffic due to the European cholera pandemic of 1892, which claimed more than a quarter of a million lives in Russia, and had severe consequences in Hamburg where 8,600 people died. This was the last serious European cholera outbreak, as cities improved their sanitation and water systems, the common source of such infections. Just two cases of cholera were identified in Jewish transmigrants waiting in Glasgow for onward travel to New York and the patients

Anchor Line: Third Class "This accommodation is exceedingly well lighted and ventilated, and fitted up in rooms, married couples, single women and single men being berthed separately and every comfort and attention is furnished that is possible on an ocean steamer. Third-class passengers are provided, free of charge, with a mattress, bedding, mess tins (plate, mug, knife, fork, spoon and water can). Tables are set for meals, and passengers are waited upon by stewards who take care of eating utensils. A liberal supply of provisions, properly cooked, will be served on the steamers three times a day by the steamers' stewards; breakfast at 9, dinner at 1, supper at 6 o'clock. £7 with cheap rail fares from other British cities." (1902)

were taken to Belvedere Hospital. The two travellers made a quick recovery, though missing their booked passage. The presence of typhus on an immigrant ship, also in 1892, caused the whole vessel to be quarantined in New York while the cholera outbreak there, which produced many fatalities, was traced back to Russia. This caused the temporary suspension of migration from the cholera areas in Russia and Germany to the United States with a consequent major effect on trans-Atlantic shipping. Patterns of travel for Jewish migrants changed substantially.

Indeed, the numbers entering America fell by about half in the following few years while competition between shipping companies increased. Between 1870 and 1892 almost 100,000 people, about a third of whom were Jewish, travelled from Hamburg to Leith and then mostly proceeded to Glasgow for onward migration to North America. Only around two thousand aliens still passed through Leith annually from the early 1900s but Glasgow still attracted large numbers of transmigrants. In 1902, for example, 2,056 reached Glasgow from Hull by train for onward travel to the United States, a number which reached 6,394 in 1906 and 9,410 the following year. Victorian train services proved very adaptable, and travellers from Hull to Glasgow were efficiently carried by North Eastern Railways. While the Glasgow numbers were much less than the approximately

The Leith Hull and Hamburg Steam Packet Company Limited.

German Billboard advertising the Leith and Hamburg Steam Packet Company sailings between Hamburg and Leith with a single fare costing £2.50. Actually, these advertised sailings did not take place because of the outbreak of World War I.

60,000 who travelled annually through Liverpool, Glasgow was the main alternative for trans-Atlantic travel though, as we have noted, there were other nationalities now being carried on the Scottish shipping lines.

Some arrivals in Glasgow had fallen foul of American health regulations. From 1898 health inspections at Ellis Island, New York, included eye examinations looking for trachoma. Those deemed likely to have the disease had to be returned to the last European post of embarkation and some hundreds were sent back across the Atlantic. As many ships had called in at a number of ports on their way to New York the precise port to which returnees should be sent could be difficult to determine but Glasgow certainly received some of these travellers.

One major social problem related to the mass migration concerned family separation. Sometimes the breadwinner travelled first to establish himself before sending for the family. Occasionally, the family reunited in Glasgow only for the breadwinner to set off alone for the United States. Jewish charitable bodies, especially the Boards of Guardians, had to help such stranded family members, often providing financial help with steamer fares. In fact, the Glasgow Jewish community had been helping stranded transmigrants from the 1860s. A more contentious issue related to return migration. In London the Jewish Board of Guardians was responsible for the return of 50,000 Jews to Eastern Europe between 1880 and 1914 in an attempt to reduce anti-Jewish prejudice and reduce the charge on their charitable funds. There was no movement of this kind from Scotland with those few returning to Russia said to be doing so of their own choosing.

The anti-immigration climate of the time, led to the setting up in 1902 of the Royal Commission on Alien Immigration, whose report resulted in the 1905 Aliens Act. Jewish community leaders from Glasgow gave positive evidence about conditions in the city's immigrant areas. The Aliens Act gave Government

Inspectors the power to exclude paupers, unless they could prove that they were entering the country solely to avoid persecution or punishment on religious or political grounds or for an offence of a political nature. When the Liberals came in to power in 1906 they did not repeal the Act, but they did not rigorously enforce it either, and the number of actual exclusions was relatively small.

Patterns of Migration

One way to track the Jewish migration is to follow larger families as they travelled from Russia on their way westward. The 1891 Census indicates that around a third of firstborn Jewish children had been born in Glasgow, a similar proportion to those born in Russia. The Glasgow born element naturally rises with the younger children but the proportion born en route through

GEOGRAPHICAL ORIGINS OF SCOTLAND'S JEWS

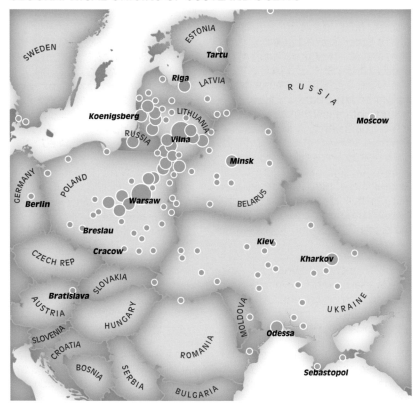

This map indicates the place of parents' marriage for first Scottish births to Jewish migrants: 1841-1901 (Details courtesy Michael Tobias)

KEY: ● *Under 10 marriages*   ● *10-49 marriages*   ● *50 or more marriages*

JEWISH CHILDREN BORN IN SCOTLAND

Census Year	1841	1851	1861	1871	1881	1891	1901	1911
Total born in Scotland	141	83	147	251	516	811	2306	3145
% under 10 years	60.3	88.0	83.0	84.1	91.5	91.9	93.9	91.2

This table shows the number of Jewish children born in Scotland and the percentage of those under the age of 10 years when first recorded in a Census. The remarkably high proportion of young children may reflect both the transitory nature of the Scottish Jewry before the First World War and the relative youthfulness of those prepared to uproot themselves and move on in search of economic security and personal safety for themselves and their families. (Courtesy: Gillian Raab and Michael Tobias)

Germany and England also increases. Place of marriage is naturally a great indicator of the areas in Eastern Europe from which the Scottish population derives. Scottish birth certificates, with data collected up to 1901, indicate the dates and places of parents' marriage. Specific locations could be identified in around 90% of 627 weddings held outside the UK, referring to 158 different towns. This map shows that Jews reached Scotland from the Baltic countries all the way south to Odessa and the Black Sea. Contemporary reports, confirmed by study data, show that more prosperous Jews were arriving from Moscow and St Petersburg during the 1890s as permits for Jewish residency were abruptly withdrawn. Prior to the 1880s, the vast majority of the migrants hailed from towns in modern Poland and Lithuania. There are a very few references to towns in present day Belarus and Ukraine before the 1880s and then only a handful in the 1880s, while the numbers increase significantly in the 1890s. Thus, the bulk of Jews arriving in Scotland in the last decades of the nineteenth century hailed from a wide area forming a rough arc, stretching from central and eastern Poland, through western Belarus and the length of Lithuania to the Baltic Sea.

The main centres for marriage locations beyond the British Isles were Warsaw, Vilna (Vilnius), Kovno (Kaunas) and Riga, while Odessa became significant only from 1891. However, more than 300 marriages of Jewish couples living in Glasgow took place in England further confirming the geographical mobility of the times.

During the main period of immigration Jewish marriages were all conducted through the various Scottish synagogues which were all under Orthodox auspices, and all weddings should have been registered with the Chief Rabbi and the London Beth Din. Between 1880 and 1901, though with some gaps in the records, only 419 Jewish Marriages in Scotland were registered in London. However, the study revealed some 558 Scottish Statutory Marriage records, for the same period, claiming to be the product of a Jewish

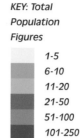

Distribution of Jews in Glasgow in 1881 (above) and 1901 (below) by Census enumeration districts.

Red and grey mark the heaviest concentration of Jewish residents, in the Gorbals and the adjoining neighbourhoods just to the north of the River Clyde.

(Courtesy: Michael Tobias)

marriage ceremony. Rabbi Abraham Shyne, rabbi of the immigrant community in the Gorbals for twenty years, was known to have carried out weddings and divorces without recourse to the London Beth Din. Furthermore, the London Beth Din issued a rebuke to him for this practice. Such wedding registration would have been unknown in the Russian Empire and might have been seen as unnecessary bureaucracy for a couple uncertain that Scotland was their final destination. It follows that up to a quarter of Scottish Jewish marriages, known in Yiddish as *stille chupas*, were conducted without proper authorisation.

Rabbi Abraham Shyne came from Helsinki to Glasgow serving as the Gorbals rabbi for twenty years from 1885.

Glasgow's population grew rapidly during the nineteenth century as its shipbuilding and heavy engineering industries expanded, and its merchant classes prospered on the back of international trade which included the growth of the textile industry and the manufacture of tobacco products. Urbanisation was a Scottish wide phenomenon creating opportunities for the newcomers not just in Glasgow but also in Edinburgh, the administrative centre of the country, Dundee, Aberdeen and other smaller towns. As the main opportunities for manufacture and trade existed in Victorian Glasgow it was only to be expected that most of the migrants would settle in the city and work in the growing textile and furniture factories as well as in a myriad of small workshops where workers might dream of becoming their own bosses.

Jewish Occupations

The study examined the occupations of the Jews living in Glasgow. In 1841 and 1851 the predominant occupations were described as merchants or agents, usually dealing in goods demanded by Glasgow's developing middle class, clothing, furs and jewellery. In 1861 there are a number of watchmakers but from 1871 the pattern changes. There are more tailors which became the dominant occupation from 1881. After 1891 there was a major move into trades associated with the tobacco industry, production and sales, with almost a fifth of the Glasgow Jews occupied in this way.

The development of peddling or hawking as a means of making business contacts and establishing the possibility of setting up in business, whether in Glasgow or beyond became a common form of occupation from 1881. The presence of Jews as market stall-holders was already receiving unwelcome attention in the 1880s. Small shop-keeping in the Gorbals became significant by 1891. About a third of the shops were butchers, bakers and grocers supplying kosher food to the Jewish population. At the same time, the category of travellers, hawkers, and pedlars was the largest in the Gorbals just exceeding the number of tailors who still numbered around a third. As late as 1911 the number of Jewish pedlars, hawkers or travellers in Glasgow numbered 541 indicating the persistence and endurance of this precarious way of life.

Peddling such items as linens and picture frames around mining communities led to the wider dispersal of Jews across Scotland. David Daiches described the *trebblers,* the travellers who sold their wares round the Fife mining towns and who spoke an odd amalgam of Scots and Yiddish, in his memoir of his Edinburgh life, *Two Worlds: An Edinburgh Jewish Childhood.* Eventually, these men became financially secure enough to set up their own businesses in Edinburgh or perhaps in Dunfermline which was closer to their customers. The Falkirk community benefitted from its proximity to the Stirlingshire coalfields while pedlars based in Glasgow travelled down to Ayrshire mining towns. A few Jews lived for a while in Cumnock maintaining contact with the Glasgow community. Gradually Jews were to be found in many parts of the countryside, owning general stores or just continuing to peddle their wares on extended credit to mining families. It was often asserted that peddling or hawking remained a major Jewish occupation in Glasgow and Edinburgh into the twentieth century, long after it had declined in the major centres in England.

Jewish occupational status changed markedly during the nineteenth century. The Census of 1891 sheds an interesting insight into immigrant life. In the Glasgow Gorbals fully one third were involved in tailoring while just over a third were described as travellers, hawkers or pedlars. Just over a tenth were involved in other manufacturing trades which included some slipper makers and picture-framers and a similar number were small shopkeepers, some supplying kosher food while others were jewellers or drapers. A decade later there were fewer people involved in the picture frame trade and more people working with tobacco. Jewish working conditions came to the attention of the *Lancet's* survey of health in the tailoring industry during 1888 but the Glasgow workshops compared favourably with those in other centres.

Such a professional element as existed was composed mainly of the various ministers of religion. There were just a few medical practitioners in Glasgow and Edinburgh from the middle of the nineteenth century but their numbers only became significant in the twentieth century. Thus, the 62 medical workers identified in the 1911 Census included thirty medical students as well as the first four Jewish doctors to remain to practise in Scotland. Less predictably, the community included blacksmiths, tinsmiths, bricklayers, coal merchants, a postman and a golf club maker. One woman, Martha Green, was identified as a nut cutter in a biscuit factory.

Business card for a Jewish tailoring company already in business before
the major immigration to Scotland began.

Groups of workers sometimes travelled together to Scotland. In
around 1870 the Glasgow business Arthur & Co brought some Jewish tailors, from
London and Amsterdam, to introduce new methods of garment production.
A company donation to the synagogue suggests that these workers were
probably recruited by a Jewish employee. In future years Arthur & Co was to be
one of the leading firms in supplying goods on credit to Glasgow-based pedlars
travelling out to mining communities. A young Jewish manager with Imperial
Tobacco in Glasgow, Lemberg (Lvov) born Jacob Kramrisch, even managed to
recruit cigarette workers directly from Poliakoff's factory in Warsaw between
1888 and 1894. By this time the tobacco trade was recognised as a major
employer within the Jewish community, accepted as respectable for Jewish
girls. Cigarette work declined after Kramrisch was promoted to a position at
the company's Nottingham headquarters and by 1911 the number of Jews
in tobacco-related work had dropped off considerably. Another factory group
recruited directly from outside Scotland were the *shmeerers* in Edinburgh,
the raincoat water-proofers for the Caledonian Rubber Company in the Dalry
district, whose unpleasant work kept them separate in their own Dalry Hebrew
Congregation from the main community for a generation.

From the last quarter of the nineteenth century until just after the
First World War Jewish agents were active in the northern fishing ports, such
as Aberdeen, Fraserburgh and Peterhead. Much of the trade concerned the

JEWISH OCCUPATIONS IN SCOTLAND 1841-1911

Census Year	1841	1851	1861	1871	1881	1891	1901	1911
Total with occupation	112	86	69	200	362	707	2013	1775
	%	%	%	%	%	%	%	%
Tailoring	1.8	0.0	7.2	4.0	22.4	19.1	22.2	27.9
Pedlars, hawkers, and travellers	8.0	11.6	15.9	16.5	27.1	33.5	19.7	16.8
Dealers and shopkeepers	18.8	17.4	24.6	12.5	9.9	9.5	7.9	9.1
Cigarette manufacture	0	0	1.4	0.5	0.3	2.0	13.4	1.1
Makers of cabinets, shoes, boots and other products	1.8	7.0	0	2.5	1.9	1.6	7.8	10.4
Jewellers and watchmakers	8.9	9.3	10.1	6.5	5.5	5.1	3.4	1.8
Waterproof makers	0	0	0	0	2.5	6.6	2.0	0.8
Other occupations	60.7	54.7	40.6	57.5	30.4	22.6	23.6	31.9

This table shows the number of adult males by occupation group in the different Census years and indicates the percentage in each of these groups. Before the arrival of significant numbers of Jews after 1881, adults in the smaller Jewish community were employed in a wide variety of merchant trades. As numbers increased from 1881 a major concentration could be seen in such activities as peddling, tailoring and other forms of manufacture. The table also shows the short-lived presence of the community of Edinburgh Jews, living in the Dalry district and with their own separate synagogue, engaged in water-proofing around 1891. Around the same time, cigarette manufacture was an important source of employment for Jews in Glasgow. (Courtesy: Gillian Raab and Michael Tobias) import of salted herring into Poland, a staple of the Jewish diet in Eastern Europe but also popular with Polish Catholics who abstained from meat on Fridays. Jews were involved at all stages of the export of herring from Scotland and its distribution from the Baltic ports and it remained popular in their diet in Scotland. As the Scottish Jewish writer, Chaim Bermant, recalled:

> 'On Sunday one had a pickled herring, on Monday soused herring, on Wednesday baked herring, on Thursday herring fried in oatmeal and Friday herring in sour cream.'

Barney Covitz, (1913-1997) ran a Shetland Pony stud farm near Coatbridge where there were usually around thirty ponies. His father had been a pony breeder in Lithuania before arriving in Scotland in 1902. Initially, his ponies were coal-mine ponies and in later years he had the best pedigree ponies in the country. He judged Shetlands at agricultural shows and in 1977 one of his foals won a first prize at the Royal Highland Show. Religiously observant he gave many of his mares Jewish names and often spoke to his ponies in Gaelic.

Dispersal around Scotland

The Censuses confirm the pattern of dispersal, the precarious nature of such enterprises and the isolation of many immigrant families away from the bigger communities where Jewish life and the Yiddish language provided a bulwark of stability. Contemporary records indicate that the pressures of work took their toll on religious observance with the Shabbat weekly holiday particularly under threat.

By 1891 there were already thirty-six Jews in Greenock, enough to establish a community in 1894. By 1901 there were sixty-two Jews in the town, numbers increasing to over one hundred and ten a decade later. Greenock, as a small port city, was the last Scottish place of embarkation before the Atlantic crossing though almost all Jews sailing to North America left from Glasgow. Greenock's growth was related to the advantages of being a busy commercial town, near enough to Glasgow, with opportunities for independent trading. Figures indicate that almost all Jews crossing the Atlantic did so from Glasgow and only about 245 Jews set sail across the Atlantic from Greenock between 1892 and 1924. In fact, most trans-Atlantic passengers from Greenock were native Scots. One enduring port myth has been the story of people deciding to disembark from the migrant vessels in Glasgow or Greenock. North Sea shipping invariably arrived at East Coast ports and Glasgow and Greenock were ports of embarkation and certainly not of arrival from Continental Europe.

Atlantic steamer schedules were not closely linked to North Sea crossings and it was not unusual for transmigrants to have to wait a couple of weeks in temporary accommodation before embarking for New York. At the other extreme before the tightening of Health Regulations some transmigrants arrived in Leith, travelled by train to Glasgow and boarded ship for the USA having spent less than a day in Scotland. Crucially, there was a Jewish hostel in Glasgow for the travellers, protecting the migrants from the petty criminals who preyed on gullible travellers. Glasgow health inspectors regularly inspected transit passengers as the docks area was often the focus of serious infections.

One of the most enduring of these small regional communities was formed in Ayr around 1901 when there were thirty-four Jews. The community grew to sixty-five in 1911 and developed an impressive network of societies and activities. As a popular resort town just thirty miles from Glasgow Ayr benefitted from regular holiday visitors. Kosher guest houses catered to holiday makers and wartime evacuees swelled the numbers which gradually fell again after the War. The community's hotel and synagogue closed during the 1970s.

We have noted the attraction of the Scottish mining communities for Jewish pedlars. For some, it was easier to live nearer the source of their income than to make lengthy daily train or bus journeys and pockets of Jewish life appeared round the countryside. Different Censuses indicate that there were Jews in small numbers, probably just a family or two around Ayrshire in such places as Cumnock, Auchinleck, Kilmarnock, Stevenston and Newmilns. There were, for example, nineteen Jews in Stevenston, a small mining centre near Saltcoats, in 1901 but a decade later only four remained. These locations, and the others in Stirlingshire and Fife, were well placed for the mining communities though the travelling salesmen would still have to make the journey to credit wholesalers in Glasgow or Edinburgh to buy the supplies required by the miners' families.

One of the Jewish pedlars in Falkirk was Gershon Spilg, who had arrived in the Gorbals in 1885. In around 1903 a couple of men from Falkirk offered him the job of minister/*shochet* for the sixteen families then living in the town at a salary of around £1.25 a week. Spilg had already served as minister/*shochet* in Greenock and he augmented his meagre salary by peddling drapery goods in the nearby villages of Polmont and Redding and further money came from a weekly chess column in the local newspaper. While *Jewish Chronicle* reports indicate that these small regional communities were usually founded by more than a dozen families, Census returns indicate that these comprised only around thirty individuals, presumably young small families, not yet having older children, who might have found the better Jewish facilities of Edinburgh or Glasgow more welcoming.

The Jewish community in Aberdeen formally established their synagogue in 1893 though most of their members had been present in the city for some years and had hesitated about making their presence public. Individual Jews and families had been living and working in the city for some decades but it was the notice attracted by the new synagogue which led to a famous court case. Within weeks of the opening of the synagogue, the local branch of the Society for the Prevention of Cruelty to Animals took the synagogue chairman, Alexander Zamek, and the minister/shochet, Rev James Littman, to court after the first shechita in the Aberdeen abattoir. Though the case against Zamek was dismissed, and that against the minister found to be not proven, there were allegations of anti-Semitism especially as the Swiss plebiscite, which led to the banning of shechita there, had taken place just weeks before the Aberdeen case. Following the trial matters settled and Jewish community life in Aberdeen continued unhindered.

The impetus to move beyond the crowded streets of the Glasgow Gorbals, where competition for work was intense, was the spur motivating members of the Greenwald family to reach the Shetlands in 1918. Eventually setting up a successful general store in Lerwick the Greenwalds managed to maintain their Jewish identity on the Shetlands through three generations as a single family within a very distinctive culture. Jews were now dispersed in many centres around Scotland but the pull of the larger cities, with their established communities, remained a powerful factor in attracting the newcomers.

Woolf Greenwald's first shop, and H&J Greenwald Department Store 1990, Lerwick, Shetlands.

The Great Migration

IDENTITY & ACCULTURATION 1880–1914

The major wave of migration which passed through Scotland around the turn of the twentieth century brought to the country the first significant non-Christian minority, different not just in religion but also in language and customs. The reception of the Jewish newcomers varied from the welcome from senior civic and religious figures who recognised the extent of Jewish suffering in Tsarist Russia to the fear and suspicion expressed by a variety of different groups. Jews also faced the intrusive and deeply resented presence of Christian missionaries, both in Glasgow and Edinburgh, themselves often of Jewish birth, who offered health care and material advancement in return for 'salvation'.

Many immigrant accounts indicate the financial pressure to work on Shabbat, the Jewish day of rest. There was also a struggle to be allowed to work on Sunday instead of Saturday, given the strict Sabbath trading laws then in force. The need to learn English was also a major imperative and classes provided by the Jewish Literary Societies, active in both Glasgow and Edinburgh, and by Glasgow's education department were well attended. While Yiddish was the *lingua franca* of the newcomers, and remained so for some decades, with Yiddish newspapers, shop-fronts and billboards in the Gorbals there was pressure to move the community to use of English as its first language. In 1892 Rev Simeon Singer had exhorted the Glasgow community to exchange their language for that of their neighbours calling Yiddish a mixture of bad German and bad Hebrew'. The Glasgow Talmud Torah, the main provider of out-of-school-hours primary Jewish education, switched from Yiddish to English as the language of instruction in 1908, a move recognised at the time as a major impetus to acculturation.

Rabbi Salis Daiches, who arrived in Edinburgh as community rabbi in 1919, saw his goal as the synthesis of Jewish and Scottish culture, a mixture of rabbinic tradition and the modern secularism. As a German university graduate, with a doctorate in the philosophy of the Scottish enlightenment, he was uncomfortable with the folksy, simplistic and often superstitious piety of the newcomers and promoted the idea of living simultaneously in the two worlds of Jewish and Scottish life, a theme portrayed beautifully in his son David's memoir *Two Worlds*. Unfortunately, the loss of piety was often associated with loss of Jewish identity both in the community and even within his own family. *Two Worlds* also illustrates that while Rabbi Daiches adhered to a rigidity of belief he made compromises in observance that he felt was in keeping with modernity, such as the use of electricity on Shabbat and a loosening of kashrut restrictions while on holiday. David recalled in an essay, printed in later editions of *Two Worlds*, that during a holiday in the Highlands Rabbi Daiches came across a tailor, living in Wester Ross, far from any Jewish community, whose only languages were Yiddish and English. This he indicated was not the synthesis he sought as no Jew could function outwith the boundaries and facilities of a Jewish community and certainly not in what he called the 'ghetto language'.

Rabbi Dr Salis Daiches (1880-1945)

Rabbi of the Edinburgh Hebrew Congregation and a leading spokesman on Jewish issues in Scotland in the inter-war years.

Formation of Community

The formation of community was therefore a crucial factor in Jewish settlement in Scotland. In the middle of the nineteenth century the Censuses indicate that the number of Jews outside the two communities of Edinburgh and Glasgow consistently number less than fifty individuals and these numbers hardly increased as the number of Jews in Scotland dramatically expanded after 1881. Thus, there were only sixty-three Jews living outside existing communities, or places where communities would be established, in 1891 and only fifty-six a decade later representing less than 1% of Scotland's Jews.

Community represented stability and an ability to adapt to Scottish ways while supported by the customs and traditions which had governed life in Eastern Europe, known affectionately, despite the poverty and backwardness it came to represent, as *der heim*. Societies for the poor, the sick, penniless brides, pauper funerals existed along with facilities for the study of Jewish texts, for kosher food and religious services. All the communities throughout

Scotland, no matter how small, maintained religion classes for their children. Cultural activities and Zionist societies existed from Inverness to Ayr and more successful members were usually ready to help impoverished arrivals. In Edinburgh community leadership was traditionally based within the Edinburgh Hebrew Congregation. In Glasgow the many different religious, cultural, social and welfare organisations came together in the Glasgow Jewish Representative Council. The Council was founded in 1914 to support the interests of the Jewish community and represent it in the wider Scottish society. It continued in this role until Scottish devolution in 1999 led to the formation of the Scottish Council of Jewish Communities which replaced the Scottish Jewish Standing Committee which had been formed more than a decade earlier.

In Glasgow and Edinburgh there were small groups of men, educated in some of the great Lithuanian *yeshivot*, who gathered to learn Talmudic lore. The Great Synagogue in Glasgow had further groups studying *mishnayot* and midrashic literature, less challenging than the Talmud but still requiring a background in serious Jewish learning. Similar Talmudic learning was also available in Edinburgh and the immigrant generation overcame their suspicions of Rabbi Daiches, as a rabbi with a PhD did not seem completely kosher to them, until they realised that he possessed serious traditional scholarship too. More 'enlightened' material was also available to the newcomers. The library in Glasgow's Great Synagogue even included modern literature in Hebrew, such as a translation of Jules Verne's *Twenty Thousand Leagues under the Sea*, published in Warsaw in the 1870s.

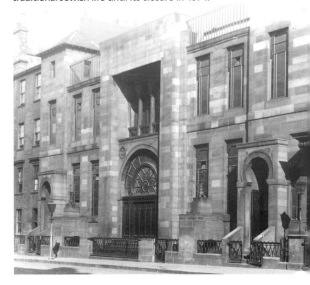

The Great (later Great Central) Synagogue in the Gorbals, Glasgow, which was also known simply as the South Portland Street Synagogue, was the centre of traditional Jewish life until its closure in 1974.

The larger communities had their own Jewish Board of Guardians which often struggled to raise the funds to cope with the needs of the newcomers, especially during the years of mass immigration. The origins of these societies can be traced back to 1838 in Edinburgh and probably just a few years later in Glasgow when it was recorded that such a body was in existence by 1845. While the Glasgow Jewish Board of Guardians provided a safety net for the poorer newcomers there were concerns that their charity was handed out in a fairly paternalistic and heavy handed manner. Consequently, more community based charities sprang up, especially in the Gorbals, providing dowries for brides, free loans for aspiring businessmen, food and fuel for the poor and 'fresh air holidays' for slum children. These societies claimed to meet the needs of the Yiddish speakers in a form they recognised and many of these were gradually subsumed into the Board of Guardians in later years.

In addition, a network of Jewish Friendly Societies developed in Glasgow and Edinburgh, usually affiliated to national Jewish organisations, which provided health and welfare services funded by society members from their weekly subscriptions. Jewish Friendly Society members could thus provide for themselves in times of illness, unemployment and bereavement without having the need for recourse to the Board of Guardians. In the smaller communities, charitable support for the needy was often a function of the synagogue, or at least its wealthier members.

Members of the Odessa Lodge Friendly Society in Glasgow, around 1910. Colourful rituals, smart uniforms and health and welfare provision made friendly societies a vital part of community life. Many of these lodges were named for figures of local or national importance while the Odessa Lodge reflected the common geographical origins of its members.

A further stimulus to the Jewish communities to enhance their welfare services was the presence of Christian missionary groups offering medical consultations, free medicine dispensaries and free hospital admissions. Missionary groups operated in both Edinburgh and Glasgow, where there was a

Hebrew Christian Synagogue, though with little ever achieved to show for their activities. The award of a knighthood to the apostate Edinburgh missionary Leon Levison at the end of the First World War caused outrage in the Jewish community and missionary activities soured relations with the Churches.

The Bonar Medical Mission, operating in Glasgow early in the twentieth century, noted in 1909 that:

> ...the presence of a substantial Jewish community was a challenge to the whole Christian community of Glasgow. The invasion of our country by a large alien population was a new phase in our national life and the Church could not stand idly by if the country was to remain a Christian country.

Such strident attitudes were not common. The mainstream churches, both the Church of Scotland and the Roman Catholic Church were sympathetic to the newcomers and also supported measures for Jewish relief in Russia. There were complaints of certain housing factors making difficulties for the Jews in the private rented sector which controlled most of the housing stock in the Jewish immigrant areas. In professional life there were claims that Jewish lawyers could not easily find legal apprenticeships in Scottish practices and the leading hospitals were slow to offer positions to Jewish doctors. In later years there were further indications that Jews were being prevented from owning properties in the Glasgow suburb of Newton Mearns and certain tennis and golf clubs did not admit Jewish members. This last was the catalyst for the acquisition of a Jewish golf club at Bonnyton Moor near Eaglesham. Chaim Bermant once recounted in *Coming Home* that a fellow pupil at Queens Park Secondary School described a teacher as being anti-Semitic for saying that Jewish pupils were particularly prone to lateness. Bermant, who was a frequent latecomer himself and used to anti-Semitism in Latvia and Lithuania, remarked that 'if that was anti-Semitism he could live with it'.

Educational Achievements

With the second generation and the secure acquisition of English the scene was set for major educational achievement. While, for some, educational access was limited by family poverty and sometimes the loss of breadwinners, especially to tuberculosis, Scottish education, with its Carnegie Grants, opened up the world of higher education to the immigrants' children. There were enough Jewish students at the Universities of Edinburgh and Glasgow to form their societies before the First World War as the first generation of Jews educated in Scotland began to enter university, mainly studying medicine.

With the wave of major immigration some of the Jews in Scotland were able to enter university after just a few years in the country. Typical of these was Dr Meyer Mann, son of Rev Jacob Mendel Teitelmann, chazzan in Edinburgh, who obtained a university place after arriving in Scotland only a couple of years earlier. Children of Jewish clergy in Glasgow entering medicine was also relatively common and Leo Glushak and Solomon Bridge were early examples. Noah Morris, later first Jew to become a Regius Professor in Scotland, had noted before the First World War that many of the Jewish students then at Glasgow University were recent refugees. From the 1920s the children of the immigrants, and predominantly at first the men, were to enter higher education in substantial numbers.

Jewish identity was also tested during the First World War as the Russia that the newcomers had fled from was allied to Britain and France in their struggle with Germany and Austria-Hungary. Jews were joining the British Army even before conscription was introduced in 1917 and indeed high profile religious services were held in synagogues in Glasgow and Edinburgh during 1916, in the presence of military top brass, to emphasise the Jewish contribution to the war effort.

Jewish soldiers gather together in Edinburgh during the First World War to emphasise the loyalty of Scotland's Jews to the war effort.

Elimelech Berislavsky's Story

1903-1904

These excerpts, from the account of Elimelech Berislavsky's journey to Glasgow, and his first experiences of the city, are a unique memoir of migration and settlement in the city during the period of the great migration. These recollections illustrate many of the themes developed in the study and indicate many of the common experiences of the journey to Scotland and the first steps of a single immigrant to adjust to the new environment.

It naturally follows, that when I mentioned this matter (of becoming an artisan) to my dear mother, she at once agreed. Of course, she would rather have seen me become a Rabbi. But when we talked the matter over quietly, she said, 'Yes, my dear son! You are right, you should start some profession or trade. But you must go back to yeshiva for another year or two.'

Choosing Glasgow

'Where do you want to go?' He asked without any preliminaries. 'My intention is to go to America', I replied. 'Oh! To America!' 'You know America is a pretty big place, name a town, or province'. I did not know. He came to my help himself. 'You want to go to New York?' 'All right' I said, 'I will go to New York'. 'This will cost you 120 Roubles'.

I quickly ran through my financial position in my mind, and I realised at once, that America is out of the question. I did not mince any matters, and told him, that I have not got that sum. 'In that case', he replied. 'I can send you to Glasgow for sixty Roubles'. I took out sixty Roubles, I counted the money twice, and handed it to him.

Coming out from the agent's house, my brother got hold of me and began to shout and rebuke me… 'All the time you kept on saying you are going to America, and all of a sudden it is Glasgow! I don't understand you at all. Surely, there is a great difference between the two places?'

'Now, about Glasgow, I can tell you it is all the same to me. Glasgow or New York. I have no relatives in either town. No particular job is awaiting me in either of these places. I shall have to struggle in any of them just the same. So what difference does that make? The only chief thing is the departure, the escape from this wretched country. As long as this is accomplished, I am satisfied.' 'Yes! You are right, my brother said.'

The Agent

I left the agent in good spirits. I took in the position at a glance. I realised that this man, acting in the way he does, must be taken up by his word, and by his word alone. He is certainly not in a position to issue written documents. His business must be conducted with the least possible incrimination to himself. As for his integrity and honesty he must rely on his customers, to whom he is responsible, otherwise, he would not be able to maintain his position for any length of time. And as all enquiries about this person was to his credit, I had no doubt whatever, that I am safe in his keeping. Besides, I came to the conclusion, and very logically too, that if I had any documents of from such a person they would be incriminating to myself, as well as to him, since the whole business was entirely illegal.

The Journey Begins

I examined my ticket. There were a few stations printed on it, of which I have never heard. But at the end in bold type was printed Warsaw. So apparently, I am going to Warsaw. I was glad of the fact. For this was a well-known big Jewish town ...

As I was about to leave, my hotel keeper rushed down, and insisted to take me to the station. He would not dream, of letting me go like this by myself. He refused any payment for his troubling about me. He was very glad, he said, to have been of some service to me. We went to the station in his own private cab. We had about an hour or so, to ourselves, and that honest and good man, was talking nothing else but my affairs. He managed to procure for me two addresses to some Glasgow people, in case I had nowhere to go to. He gave me all kinds of instructions and asked me to be very careful. His behaviour towards me was like from a father to a son. At last arriving at the station, I said goodbye to him, and went straight for my platform.

The night was bitterly cold. I was hungry. I was very tired ... When the first bell rang I jumped on the train. I was not long on it, when I noticed a crowd of emigrants, one could not mistake them. They had such a worn out look about them. They had a lot of big bundles with them, bed clothing, and all kinds of menagerie. When the conductor came in, there was a great commotion. He wanted them to remove all the bundles to the luggage van. After some heated altercations and some money being passed from hand to hand, quietness was restored again. The majority were Jewish people, travelling for days and days, perhaps weeks, and going to all corners of the Globe, some to America, others to the Argentine, some going so far as China.

Crossing the Border

'Quiet!' the man commanded. 'We are taking you over the frontier this afternoon. Be ready and calm'. Taking a bundle of papers, he began to make explanations, giving everyone a passport under fictitious names. We raced, we jumped and did all sorts of tricks, in a few minutes we could see the frontier. There was a bridge. By this bridge were stationed a few soldiers. A chain was thrown across the road. When we came up, the soldiers stood at attention. An officer came up, inspected everyone's passport, and asked the names. When my turn came, he gave me a passport and told me to be very careful, not to forget that my name is now 'Abraham Shavriner'. I got hold of this document, examined it carefully. These were passports with monthly dates only. Well, I thought, this will do very nicely, since I only required it for a few hours. We were told to guard these documents very carefully, as we will have to return them as soon as we crossed the frontier.

I passed through. In a few minutes the whole party numbering about fifteen went through the barrier without a hitch. On the other side, the German frontier and custom was disposed of in a similar manner. Our luggage was inspected, the only thing remained was to celebrate this most eventful act by a cheap sort of German whisky. I did not like it at all, but drank it all the same. We were not long there. Our agent soon appeared on the scene, and very cautiously collected all the passports and departed.

To me, going to cross the frontier like proper citizens armed with bona fide passports, this was an unexpected delight and a great relief. I heard a good many stories about crossing the frontier. Early next morning we were provided with Railway tickets to Ostrovo. Coming to this German town, we were brought to a big establishment. I had some food and drink, and then began to look around a little, and to come in conversation with the various crowds in that big hall. They were mostly Jewish people, travelling to all corners of the Globe. And nearly everyone, by some illegal agent or other. The stories I heard there, I shall never forget all my life. The same day, I made my way to the station, and we were off to Hamburg via Berlin.

In Hamburg

Coming to Hamburg, we were taken directly to the Emigration shelter. No sooner did I enter this very large hall, when an official came in, and asked me to accompany him to the office. 'Now!' One of them shouted, 'where are you going from Glasgow?' I stood bewildered! 'I am not going anywhere from there', I replied falteringly. 'From Glasgow you are going to New York!' he shouted, 'I know you can't deceive me. Have you any addresses? Show me them quickly!' I pulled out my note book, and he snatched the book from my hand, perused it. 'Oh!' he roared. 'You have addresses for New York. Now! Look here, you book here a ticket right now for New York, and be done with it, and don't try your tricks on us, for it won't do here'. 'I haven't enough money for that journey', I managed to cry out, my eyes full of tears. I emptied my pockets and gave it to the man, saying 'This is all I possess'. He counted the money, carefully and said. No! there is not enough there, you must go and see, you may be able to raise some money among your friends'. And opening the door, he pushed me out.

An old man was waiting for me outside and he explained to me afterwards the whole fraud. 'You see! It seems, there is a great competition going on among the big shipping companies, the German and English. Now, there are agents, who actually send some people via London or other English ports to America by their liners. Now these Germans got to know of this, and they are using all sorts of tricks and games to make all the emigrants travel by German liners. I call this an absolute fraud. You go in now, and demand your belongings immediately, and tell them, you have a friend outside and should they not comply with your demand that you are going straight to the police.'

Having this good man on my side, and feeling relieved from my sudden troubles, I rushed in the room to talk to them in Russian, and called them by all the names of vagabonds and scoundrels, demanded my belongings. One tall fellow came up, and shouted that he was going to send me back to Russia, as I had no passport. At this I offered to fight him on the spot, and taking off my jacket, I shouted at the top of my voice, 'Come on, you scoundrel, I will show you how to take advantage of a poor stranded emigrant.' At this the other man came quickly on the scene, gave me back all my belongings and pushed me out of the room.

I have already forgotten all about it, in my great relief. We had to wait a few days for the boat to take me to Grimsby.

Arriving in Glasgow

(In Grimsby) I was directed to my train without any difficulty, and very soon found myself in a third class compartment, travelling to Glasgow. While in the train, I counted carefully all my money, and I found I had nineteen shillings and two pence.[1] Not a very large sum indeed, to begin a new life in a strange country. I arrived in Glasgow early in January 1904. It was very foggy and cold. I was very hungry, not having had a proper meal for three days. The crossing from Hamburg to Grimsby took me about forty hours.

I fled from Russia, I left my parents and all my kindred in that land; I deserted the army. Why did I do it? Was it because I committed some crime or incurred fabulous debts? Did I hate my parents and relatives to run away from them? No, a thousand times no! I committed no crimes, I owed no one any debts, and I loved my family. But I fled the country because I had no air, no breathing space, no freedom. I was persecuted, I was insulted and assaulted, like a good many of my co-religionists, for no fault of my own. Wasn't I born and bred in that country? Why was I denied all human rights although I was a good law abiding citizen. The answer is because I am a Jew! Those barbaric nations know they can get away with it. If the Jew had his own country, his own army, guns and powder in plenty there would not be such a thing as an anti-Semite.

Central Station Glasgow as it appeared just before Elimelech's arrival in January 1904. Many Jewish migrants who arrived at such east coast ports as Leith or Dundee in Scotland or Hull or Grimsby in England arrived at this station. From here migrants could remain in the city or travel on to the United States. (Image from www.scienceandsociety.co.uk)

---

1   Equivalent to 96 pence but worth around £50 in 2015 prices.

First Steps in Glasgow

When my agent told me in Brest-Litovsk that I am to go to Glasgow, I began to make enquiries about this famous Scottish city. I was told in the first place, that salt herring you can get for one penny a pound, and sugar was three ha'pennies. Girls earn there as much as two pounds (twenty roubles) a week. Good Lord! I exclaimed! I am a man! I should easily double that. But even £2 is also not too bad; I would live on, say five Roubles a week, and save fifteen in a month. In a year, I can make a fine penny and send money to my parents.

Suddenly I came to a halt. Somebody began to talk to me in Yiddish. 'Sholom Aleichem, I see you are a greener?' I did not know the meaning of it, I looked round, looked at my clothes, they by no means looked green. He seemed to have understood me; he glanced at my address and said. 'Oh! You are on the wrong track altogether. Come with me'. He took me to a tram car, paid my fare, and told the conductor to put me down at my destination, and he vanished, without giving me even a chance to thank him. I was not long in reaching the place, it turned out to be a very poor quarter of the town, close to the Clyde.

Finding Work I

In the evening we sat down to a quiet cup of tea, and a smoke. 'What is your trade? Your occupation?' my landlord asked me.

Links warehouse, Gorbals 1907. The shop sign gives ample evidence of the familiarity of the Jewish newcomers with spoken English but illustrating their difficulty with reading and writing it. There is other evidence of advertising in English, from posters and billboards of the period, but using Hebrew characters. This shop front advertises 'Swiss Embroidered Blouse Lengths' and 'Regular Goods' in Yiddish lettering. The Links business thrived and Abraham Links became one of the community's most successful business leaders taking a major role in the Glasgow Zionist movement and becoming a prominent art patron.

'Oh! I know one or two good trades. I can do a little bookbinding, a little wheelwright craft, I can stitch on a machine'. 'That is not much good to have a few occupations', my host remarked. 'In this country, one has to work very hard to make a living, not like in Russia, where everything comes to you so naturally and easy'. My heart gave a big thump. So that is it, one has to work hard here, and I thought the opposite. The following day, I was directed to a large clothing factory. After a few commonplace words and introductions, I was placed by a machine, and told to stitch.

In this manner, I spent my time till Friday afternoon. Friday about 3pm I got up from my treadmill of a machine, and put on my coat. 'Where are you off to?' the manager accosted me. 'Oh! It is nearly Shabbos, now it is getting dark!' 'What of it?' he exclaimed! 'You are not in Russia now, landsman. You are in England, and you have to work on Shabbos. Do you understand?' 'Have you a different God in England?' I asked him in turn. 'You will not make me work on Shabbos'. 'Then you will starve!' he shouted. He ran away and came back quickly, with a small envelope. 'Here is your money, and don't come back any more', he shouted angrily. 'We have no place here for stupid greenhorns'.

Finding Work II

'Well young man! What can we do for you? You seem to be quite a healthy young man and should be able to earn your living in this free

The textile, sewing and tailoring trade was the pre-eminent Jewish immigrant form of employment. At its worst was the sweated workshop while for others it represented the first rung on the ladder out of poverty. Collins cap making factory Oxford Street, Glasgow, c1914.

country'. This was spoken in Yiddish, and left no doubt in my mind at all where I am – in a charitable institution. I must have fainted. When I came to, I found myself in the street, a man talking to me in a friendly tone. He told me he was one of the committee men of the Board of Guardians and he got a job for me, and straight away took me there. This turned out to be a small tailoring establishment. There were only three workers, and I was the fourth. On being introduced to him, he received me very friendly and when I told him, that I will not work on the Shabbos, under any circumstances, he consented immediately, and he carried out his promise to the letter. He would let me work the whole night on a Thursday, in order to facilitate my leave on Friday early in the afternoon. He did more than that, he even encouraged me, and told me how proud he was to know that he is in a position to afford me this privilege. 'You know', he said, 'I very often cry when I stand and work on the Sabbath, but I cannot help it. I have to make a living for my family. Had I been a single man, like you, I would also do the same'. I managed to save a few shillings every week, by living very frugally indeed. My earnings were about 13-14 shillings a week. And I had had to guard against slack time when I earned only about 8-9 shillings.

Settling Down and Moving On

I attended regularly the Synagogue not only for prayers, but also for the study of the Talmud. I came among all sorts of people, and when asked, what my occupation was I could not tell them that I was working at the machine. I had to evade the question.

Glasgow Yiddish newspaper November 1903: adverts offer ways of sending money to family in Russia and arrangements for helping travellers cross the Russian border.

Spring came along and I managed to stray in to the Queen's Park. Well! I was amazed. After the long dreary days with fogs and rain, and not seeing a green leaf anywhere for months and months, this was to me a veritable paradise. I stood there glued to the spot. I did not know what to admire first. I inhaled the fragrant air with my whole being. It was like Paradise. Ah! I thought, if I could only earn one pound a week, how happy I would be! Little by little, I began to settle down. Very soon I came in contact with some young people and we formed a Hebrew speaking society. In this manner the winter soon passed by, and when the Passover holiday was approaching, I felt again a great longing for home, and it took me all my strength to withstand this great longing.

The first week in August my master informed me that he is leaving Glasgow to take up a similar position in Liverpool with his brother's firm and much better prospects. He at the same time urged me to come with him, as work is waiting for him there, and he would also give me a substantial raise in my wages. I was overjoyed. I was glad to get away from that congested Scottish capital, where there was nearly always rain and fog, and practically all tenement houses, where one had to climb stairs continually. I was getting tired of it.

Postscript: Elimelech Berislavsky did not continue in tailoring. He decided that he would be better using his years of study in the yeshiva to become a community minister just as his mother had wanted. He served the small community of Llandudno in Wales for three decades, with a short early spell in Pontypridd, using the name Rev Emanuel Berry, augmenting his salary by running a guest-house, with his wife, in the popular seaside town.

Emanuel Berry (Elimelech Berislavsky) and his wife Fanny

Religion
and its
Leadership

1880-1945

Scotland's Jewish communities were served by some dozens of rabbis, cantors and ministers during the immigrant period, and their stories and experiences in the various towns and cities shed an interesting insight into both community life and how these individuals were affected by the communities they served. Many of the ministers moved around the country seeking to eke out a living serving the small town communities much as many Jews moved from place to place seeking to find somewhere they could work and bring up their family. As the Scottish communities were not seen as final destinations by most of the immigrants such movement was inevitable. Thus, some ministers, like their co-religionists, moved to different communities in Scotland, left for the bigger opportunities in England or set sail for the United States. We shall see all these options acted out by examining the careers of just some of Scotland's Jewish religious leadership in the immigrant period.

Many of the newcomers to Scotland had grown up in strictly obser-vant homes and, despite the challenges and obstacles in the way of Shabbat observance, many immigrants had the necessary skills to provide the kind of services that the small communities were looking for. Some moved out of the Jewish ministry and joined the community mainstream in terms of religious observance. In Edinburgh the descendants of Rev Fürst and Rabbi Daiches, who between them served the community in Scotland's capital for over 70 years, were to move away from their family's strict observance. However, many more, especially in Glasgow, were able to set an example of rabbinic leadership and pass their legacy to their children.

We have noted how small groupings in such places as Inverness and Falkirk could form communities with barely thirty Jews in the town and even begin to employ a minister who could lead services, teach their children and act as *shochet*, providing kosher chicken for their Shabbat meals. Salaries were minimal, reflecting the poverty-level incomes of their congregants, and though they might sometimes be supplemented by part-time commercial activities the turnover of such ministers was frequently quite rapid.

The Greenock community was one of the first to be formed in a small Scottish town though there are conflicting dates for its establishment possibility reflecting the mobile nature of its members. However, by 1894 they had appointed Gershon Spilg as their first minister. This appointment did not last very long and Spilg turned to selling goods around the Glasgow area until, as we have already seen, some ten years later he was persuaded to become the first minister in Falkirk, supplementing the meagre income by peddling goods around the local mining towns and even composing chess puzzles for the local paper. Again this appointment was short-lived and Spilg returned to Glasgow where his son Reuben, later known as Robert Spence, set up a major warehousing business. Falkirk managed to appoint further ministers, firstly Symon Gerber and a further minster during the war, who had succeeded at a military tribunal in deferring military service on the grounds that his clerical appointment had preceded the introduction of conscription.

By 1905 the Greenock community was able to appoint Rev Israel Tiemianka, who had been born in a *shtetl* near Lodz, as their minister. Tiemianka had come to London from Rotterdam where he had married in 1903. In London, he was appointed *chazzan* at the Fieldgate Street Synagogue in the East End. His move to Greenock reflected his desire to enter the ministry full-time. During his tenure in Greenock the community obtained its small cemetery and he hosted the Chief Rabbi during his visit to the town as part

Rev Gershon Spilg and the children of the Falkirk Cheder (Hebrew Classes) around 1908.

Rev Israel Tiemanka, Minister of the Greenock Hebrew Congregation. and his son Henri Tiemanka, born in Greenock, violin virtuoso in America.

of a pastoral visit to Scotland in 1906. After a short spell as a *cheder* teacher at the new Queens Park Synagogue in Glasgow Israel and Feiga Tiemianka settled in Holland, where Feiga had grown up, and where Israel became the head of the local diamond bourse. Tiemianka's son Henri was born in Greenock in 1906 and his musical talent was recognised early on. He was given a violin at the age of six and was to become one of the great violin virtuosi in America managing to use his contacts to get his parents out of Holland before the Nazi invasion.

The movement of ministers round the small communities brought Rev Samuel Arkush to Inverness. Before long he moved on to the Dalry Hebrew Congregation, the waterproofers synagogue in Edinburgh, before being appointed minister in the Queens Park Synagogue in Glasgow. Even this more significant appointment was short-lived as Arkush moved on to posts in Cardiff and Blackpool. After Arkush left Inverness he was replaced by Rev Falk who had previously been minister in Ayr. Falk proved to be an innovative teacher bringing *ivrit b'ivrit,* modern Hebrew language teaching, to the local children but did not stay long enough to assess the changes he had introduced. Falk moved on to Dundee to be replaced in turn by Rev Gerber, who had also been in one of the small synagogues in Edinburgh, and then by Rev Ticktin who had come to Inverness from Boston in Lincolnshire.

Such a rapid turnover of ministers demonstrates both the commitment made by these communities to employ religious leaders and also the poor salaries which necessitated movement to other communities in the hope of a better living or indeed into other avenues of employment. The Aberdeen community was larger than those in Dunfermline, Ayr, Inverness and Falkirk but they too had ministers who remained in town for only a short period. After the Second World War they were able, for a few years, to employ full-time ministers on a reasonable salary but their first appointment, Harry Jacobi, remained only for three years and his replacement Dr Gustav Pfingst was to die in 1957 after just a year in Aberdeen. Declining numbers during the 1950s, to around 75 members, meant that Pfingst was never replaced.

Dundee's experience was essentially different. Their first minister, Rev Simon Wulf Rosenzweig was appointed in 1893 but left for Blackpool in

1902 and there followed the usual short-term appointments for a couple of decades. In 1920 the Dundee Synagogue opened its new building with 182 seats, the largest synagogue outside Glasgow or Edinburgh. Two years later they appointed Rev M Franks who was minister until 1937 and his successor Rev M Isaacs remained in Dundee until 1944. The longest serving minister in the smaller Scottish communities was Rev Morris Segal who became the minister in Dundee in 1945. He had been minister in Dunfermline for over twenty years until the community there was dissolved and he was to serve the Dundee community for another twenty years.

In Edinburgh the community employed as its minister during the main immigrant period the Rev Jacob Fürst (1844 – 1918) who came to the city from Middlesborough in 1879. He served Edinburgh's Jews for almost

Rev Jacob Furst: minister of the Edinburgh Hebrew Congregation 1878-1918

forty years, and five of his ten children were born in the city, bringing continuity and stability to the community. His circumcision register, meticulously compiled, provides a detailed account of the males born into the community during these decades. He was prepared to stand up publicly for Jewish rights and to expose anti-Semitic attitudes leaving a model for communal leadership which was maintained by his successor, Rabbi Dr Salis Daiches. Furst arrived when the community was based at the Park Place Synagogue until the Graham Street Synagogue, a former church building, was consecrated in 1898. He proved to be acceptable to the various synagogues in Edinburgh being invited to preach at the Dalry community as well as at the synagogues on Roxburgh Place and North Richmond Street.

His son Elias Fürst was born during a family visit back to Latvia and arrived in Edinburgh at the age of six. He was a keen football supporter and was appointed as Chairman of Hearts Football Club when only thirty-nine years old, and became the first Hearts official to be elected as Chairman of the Scottish Football League. The Hearts website records that Elias' passion for football began when his father took him to matches on Shabbat, a sign that Rev Fürst was keen to ensure his children were accepted into Edinburgh life. The story sounds improbable although some football clubs open their gates about twenty minutes from the end of the game and free entry would have been possible. By the time Hearts won the Scottish Cup in 1906, Elias was allowed to display the trophy in the window of his jewellers' shop at 45 South Bridge, but despite these signs of acceptance it was said that Fürst never managed to shed his outsider status.

Rabbi Louis Rabinowitz (1906-1984) was born in Edinburgh where his father, Jacob, functioned as rabbi for a number of years. Louis Rabinowitz was rabbi in several London synagogues and during World War II he was appointed Senior Jewish chaplain of the British Army. He served with Allied forces in the Middle East and during the Normandy invasion. In 1945 Rabinowitz accepted a position as Chief Rabbi of the United Hebrew Congregations of Johannesburg and the Federation of Synagogues of Transvaal and the Orange Free State in South Africa. In the post-war period, Rabbi Cyril Harris (1836-2005) was a second Scottish-born Chief Rabbi of South Africa serving from 1987. Seen as the conscience of the Jewish community, his strong stance against apartheid raised the profile of the Jewish community during the transition to majority rule and created friendship and trust with Nelson Mandela and the new African leadership.

Fürst's successor was Rabbi Dr Salis (Bezalel) Daiches (1880-1945). Daiches was born in Vilna, the son of Rabbi Israel Hayim Daiches, who became a rabbi In Leeds after serving a community in Lithuania for a short period. Rabbi I H Daiches published many volumes of religious *responsa* and though a traditional rabbi was known for his lenient opinions, especially relating to the operation of the *mikve*, the Jewish ritual bath. Salis Daiches was educated by his father and at the Rabbinical Seminary in Berlin obtaining a PhD from the University of Leipzig in 1903 on the thought of David Hume. After serving communities in Hull and Sunderland Daiches took the post in Edinburgh in 1919 where he remained rabbi until his death in 1945.

Daiches saw his task as uniting the Jews of Edinburgh and it was at his instigation that the synagogue in Salisbury Road was built in 1932 to house all the different communities then in the city. These included the Graham Street Synagogue, seen as representing the more accultured immigrants, as well as the smaller prayer houses which were more traditional in their outlook. There had been some initial resistance to forming a unified community but his persistence, and provision of traditional learning for the more observant, gradually won the day. Daiches was widely seen as the leading spokesman for Judaism in Scotland, seeking a synthesis between Jewish and Scottish thought and eschewing the simplistic beliefs of many of his immigrant congregants. He defended Jewish interests in the public arena and was active in both B'nai B'rith and the Zionist movement, having proudly attended the opening ceremony of the Hebrew University of Jerusalem in 1925. The affectionate memoir of his son David, *Two Worlds*, relates his firm attachment to Orthodox thought combined with a more liberal attitude to many areas of religious practice. His attempts at a Scottish-Jewish synthesis, in terms of observance and belief, remained somewhat elusive and it is questionable whether it had much impact on his community or even his own family.

The formation of a unitary community in Edinburgh produced a history very different from that in Glasgow, where the community size led to a multiplicity of synagogues, and consequently of rabbis. There was a short lasting dissident independent community in Edinburgh, formed after the arrival of

Rabbi Daiches in the city. This group made the major mistake of appointing as minister the Rev Alexander Levison, a brother of Leon Levison, a Jewish convert to Christianity who headed a Medical Mission to the Jews in Edinburgh. Rabbi Daiches and the *Jewish Chronicle* were able to defend themselves in court against claims made by Rev Levison that he had received rabbinic ordination, *semicha*, from the Chief Rabbi of Palestine, Rabbi Kook, which Daiches had disputed. The case ended when Rabbi Daiches proved beyond doubt that Levison's ordination certificate had been forged. The independent community soon closed and the 'dissidents' became reconciled to Rabbi Daiches.

David Daiches described his father as the 'virtual though not nominal' leader of Scottish Jewry. While he may have had aspirations to be regarded as Scotland's senior rabbi, the existence of a traditional Beth Din in Glasgow, with its full complement of rabbinic leadership, made such an appointment impossible. However, in the eyes of Scottish civic and church society, and certainly in his own, he was Scotland's 'chief rabbi'.

Rev E P Phillips was appointed as minister to the Glasgow Hebrew Congregation in 1878 just before the community's move from George Street to the newly built Garnethill Synagogue in 1879. He was recognised by the Chief Rabbi in London as the spiritual leader of all of Glasgow's Jews and he was to involve himself in all aspects of religious leadership and was active in many of the new societies, religious, education and welfare, which sprang up in the Gorbals as the community there expanded. He took the minutes for the central Gorbals synagogue when it was based in Main Street before the Great Synagogue in South Portland Street opened in 1901. He visited Oscar Slater in jail when Slater was facing the death penalty for the murder of Marion Gilchrist, and his belief in Slater's innocence led him to take an active role

Rev E P Phillips with Oscar Slater after Slater's release from Peterhead Jail in 1927. Slater, a Jewish immigrant from Germany, had been imprisoned for twenty for a murder in Glasgow he did not commit in a major miscarriage of justice. The case still retains huge public interest.

in the campaign for his release. It was to take two decades for the Scottish legal system to admit the flaws in the case against Slater and in 1927 he was released from Peterhead Prison into Rev Phillips' care.

Phillips had been born in Adelaide, Australia in around 1855 and trained at Jews' College in London. This suited the membership at Garnethill who wanted an English speaking minister trained at a religious seminary rather than a traditional yeshiva. However, as the number of strictly observant immigrants increased and the desire for a Yiddish-speaking yeshiva-trained rabbi for the Gorbals grew it became clear that Phillips would have to accede to the need for a communal rabbi from Eastern Europe. In fact, there had been such a rabbi operating unofficially in the Gorbals from around 1886 with the arrival of Rabbi Abraham Shyne from Helsinki. Shyne never held any official position but was frequently called upon for various religious services. Shyne's readiness to by-pass British officialdom and perform religious weddings, the so-called *stille chuppes*, and divorces, *gittin*, led to reprimands from the Chief Rabbi's Beth Din in London. Shyne's wife died in 1906 but he remarried the following year and left Glasgow around 1907 to settle in Jerusalem. The way was now clear for the appointment of a Gorbals rabbi.

The choice, in March 1908, fell upon Rabbi Samuel Isaac Hillman (1868-1953). Hillman had received *semicha*, rabbinic ordination, from prominent rabbis in Ponevezh, Slutsk, Volozhin and Dvinsk, all towns in modern Belarus and Lithuania. At the age of 29 he became rabbi and head of the religious court, *beth din*, in Berazino in the Minsk Region. In his six years in Glasgow Hillman set a firm path of religious Orthodoxy having attended the inaugural meeting of the ultra-Orthodox Agudas Israel in Kattowitz in 1912. He made a major impact on the religious life of the Glasgow community, founding a local Beth Din to rule on religious issues and establishing a small yeshiva, teaching in Yiddish, to encourage traditional learning amongst the Jewish youth. His intellectual abilities and organisational strength led to his being appointed to the London Beth Din in 1914 where he served as a religious judge, *dayan*, for twenty years. On his retirement to Jerusalem he devoted himself to study and writing, producing a 20-volume commentary on every tractate of the Babylonian and Jerusalem Talmuds and many other works. He founded a yeshiva in Jerusalem with his son-in-law, the Chief Rabbi of Israel Yitzhak HaLevi Herzog, and served as its head.

Rabbi S I Hillman, rabbi of the Gorbals community 1908-1914

Hillman's son David was one of the first Jewish students at the Glasgow School of Art and he became renowned for his work in designing stained glass windows for synagogues. His artistic flair and facility with Jewish themes can be seen in numerous synagogues in London as well as at the Hechal Shlomo Jewish Heritage Centre, in Jerusalem. Rabbi Hillman did not approve of his son's study at the Glasgow School of Art and this decision caused an irreparable family rift.

As the community grew the number of synagogues in the Gorbals proliferated and the community was able to attract major rabbinic figures to the city. One such was Rabbi Yaakov Ben Zion Mendelsohn Morein (1875-1941) from Kreitzburg, in the Vitebsk region of Belarus. He received *semicha*, ordination, from the Rogatchover Gaon, one of the great rabbinic figures of the time. Shortly thereafter, he was drafted into the Russian Army but he managed to desert, changing his surname to Mendelsohn to make it harder for the Army to find him. After posts in London, Leeds and Gateshead he came to Glasgow in 1912 where his Yiddish sermons, *droshos*, were greatly valued by the poor immigrants whose causes he espoused. He served first as rabbi of the small Workingmen's Synagogue, known as Poalei Tzedek, literally Workers of Righteousness and later as rabbi of the Chevra Kadisha Synagogue where he became involved in local issues. He helped efforts to establish a Jewish home for the elderly and took active measures to reduce the price of kosher food. With the onset of the First World War, Rabbi Mendelsohn was concerned that his son Chaim might be drafted and given his own experience in the Russian Army he decided to move on to New Jersey in the United States. A talented author of Talmudic and Rabbinic works he wrote six scholarly volumes including *Midrash Yaavetz*, published in Glasgow in 1911 with an approbation from Rabbi Nosson Halevi Bamberger of Würzburg.

Rabbi Hillman's successor as Av Beth Din was Rabbi Jacob David Lurie (1869-1957) a native of Slabodka where there was a famous yeshiva and where his father was a well-known Talmudist. After serving for some years as Rosh Yeshiva in Bialystok he came to London but moved on to Hull before taking up his post in Glasgow in 1914. After a short period at the Machzikei Hadas Synagogue in the Gorbals he moved to the nearby Chevra Kadisha Synagogue where he was the rabbi for over forty years. He was widely revered for his saintly piety and despite his intellectual abilities was held in high popular regard as a 'man of the people'. His own sons, like many of their contemporaries, became doctors.

Another major rabbinic figure in Glasgow was Rabbi Benjamin Beinush Atlas, son of Rabbi Meir Atlas, a leading figure in the Lithuanian community of Shavli. Rabbi Atlas served the Great Synagogue in South Portland Street as rabbi for thirty years. With his brother-in-law Rabbi Elchonon Wasserman, widely acknowledged as one of the leading figures of Orthodoxy in the inter-war years, he brought Rabbi Naftoli Herz Shapiro to Glasgow to become head of its yeshiva. Atlas' concern for supervision of kosher meat led to his rejecting the request of Glasgow's kosher butchers to permit porging of hindquarter meat, to make it fit for kosher consumption, and following correspondence with Dayan Yechezkiel Abramsky of the London Beth Din in 1941 this view became standard British practice.

Rabbi Naftoli Shapiro (1906–1981) was born in Mir, in Poland, and studied at its prestigious yeshiva from the age of twelve. He subsequently learned at the Raduń Yeshiva, as a pupil of the saintly rabbinic figure known as the Chofetz Chaim, and at the Łomża Yeshiva, where he supervised senior students preparing for *semicha*. He arrived in Glasgow from Leeds in 1936 and went on to lead the local yeshiva for forty years. Believing that traditional Jews should also have a broad secular education he also obtained an MA from the University of Glasgow. In 1956, he was appointed rabbi of the newly amalgamated Great and Central Synagogues and he retired to Jerusalem in 1976.

The Gorbals in Glasgow even had its own Chasidic *rebbe*, Rabbi David Solomon Morgenstern, known as the sixth Kotzker Rebbe. He came to the Bais Yaakov Synagogue in Glasgow from the East End of London, where he had been naturalised as a British citizen in 1936. There had been Chasidic *sthteibles* in Glasgow since before 1913 and a group of Kotzker and Sassover Chasidim founded the Nusach Ari community which in turn amalgamated with the Bais Yaakov Synagogue. Morgenstern attracted many Chasidic visitors to Glasgow, some travelling from Poland and Lithuania to receive his blessing. The barmitzvah of his son, Israel Chaim, brought many leading figures from Eastern Europe to Glasgow in 1939. Rabbi Morgenstern eventually settled in Chicago.

As the Jewish community in Glasgow grew communities developed to the south of the Gorbals. The Queens Park Hebrew Congregation was established in 1906 and in the following year they brought Mordechai Katz (1870-1924) from Cardiff to be their rabbi, holding their first services in his home. With the rapid growth of the congregation a site in Lochleven Road was acquired and eventually an imposing building in Falloch Road was built. Rabbi Katz retired from Queens Park around 1920 moving to Ayr where his wife was running a kosher guest house. He functioned as an honorary minister there until his sudden death at the age of only 54 in 1924.

Rev Dr I K Cosgrove came from Poplar, London to become Minister of the Garnethill Hebrew Congregation and spokesman for the Jewish community to the wider society.

In 1936 Garnethill Synagogue chose Rev Dr Isaac Kenneth Cosgrove (1902-1972) then minister in Poplar in the East End of London to lead its congregation. Rev Cosgrove, who had been born in the Welsh town of Tonypandy, followed the path of Rev Phillips, representing Jewish Glasgow to the wider world while taking the lead in such matters as visiting Jewish children in the general school system, organising the provision of kosher meals to Jewish school-children, supporting sick visiting and acting as chaplain to the few Scottish Jews who found themselves to be in jail. He had been Chaplain to HM Armed Forces during the Second World War and his position as minister at Garnethill gave him leadership of the community religious issues which fell outwith the scope of the Glasgow Beth Din.

This role was to cause conflict, as we shall see, in the post-war era. His advocacy of better conditions for those in the community with learning disabilities was recognised by the formation of residential and day services provided by Cosgrove Care, and named in his honour.

Chaim Bermant's father, Rabbi Azriel Bermant, was brought to Glasgow in 1937 at the initiative of his uncle Louis Daets to be a *shochet*. Chaim described how his colleagues took him aside on arrival and told him he would need to adapt his appearance to make himself acceptable. His beard was to be trimmed and the *payot*, side curls, had to go. Further, his ability to perform rabbinical duties was hampered by the demand of the community to speak '*mit a guten Engils*' by people who were barely literate in the language. The Glasgow community made an attempt, during the Second World War to create the post of communal rabbi, in addition to the position of Rabbi Lurie as *Av Beth Din*. Thus, in 1942 Rabbi Kopul Rosen (1913-1962), later the founder of Carmel College, the Jewish boarding school in Oxfordshire, was appointed to this post serving for a couple of years before moving to a post in London.

While the Glasgow Jewish community could boast of a great array of important rabbinic figures, they did not prevent a drift from organised religious life from the 1920s. Early issues of the *Jewish Echo* in the 1930s point to the multiplicity of synagogues in the Gorbals with their empty seats. The Great Synagogue in South Portland Street recognised the emotional pull of the *chazzan*, cantor, at an early stage and in its first years employed Rev Joseph Glushak, a member of the Royal Academy of Music in Vienna. Edinburgh too employed a *chazzan* down to modern times. For an increasingly secularised membership, though reared on the traditions of Eastern Europe, it was the

Rabbi Kopul Rosen and community leaders at the opening of the Aberdeen Synagogue in 1945.

vocal ability of the *chazzan* on the High Holy Days, rather than the scholarship of the rabbi, which reconnected the immigrant Jew with the traditions from which he was becoming estranged.

The best known of Glasgow's cantors of this era was Rev Isaac Hirshow who moved from the Chevra Kadisha Synagogue in the Gorbals to Garnethill in 1925. There was a sense of pride in the Gorbals that Hirshow had been offered the post but concern that he would find the transition to the more 'English' synagogue more difficult. Garnethill had a mixed voice choir but it was open to Hirshow's plan to make synagogue worship 'beautiful and imposing'. Hirshow was to prove to be an outstanding success at Garnethill. They compromised on the important issues: 'You let me have my beard and I let you have your English'. He was Glasgow University's first Bachelor of Music graduate and he designed its blue and white graduation hood.

Simcha Kussevitsky (1906-1998) was born near Vilna, the third of four sons all noted for their exceptional cantorial skills. He and his brothers followed the family tradition of music, singing in synagogue choirs and learning perfect Hebrew pronunciation. After a short stint in the Polish army, Simcha was invited to become a *chazzan* in Rovno and he stayed there about three years. Knowledge of his singing had reached Glasgow and he became *chazzan* at the Queens Park Synagogue in 1932. Simcha left Glasgow in 1935 to become *chazzan* at the Great Synagogue, Duke's Place, London, then the 'seat' of the Chief Rabbi. After the war Simcha accepted a position at a synagogue in Greenside, Johannesburg, moving in 1952 to Cape Town, to be the cantor of the newly built Tifereth Israel Synagogue. While in London Simcha had taken part in a concert at the Royal Albert Hall in February 1946 with the London Symphony Orchestra and the following year the four brothers performed together at Carnegie Hall, New York.

Whether in the small communities or the two larger ones, Jewish religious leadership in Scotland reflected many of the trends of the narrative of Jewish migration, dispersal, settlement, onward travel, acculturation and Jewish resilience. Though the community was becoming less observant it was the Orthodox way of life which the synagogues reflected. A Reform synagogue was established in Glasgow in around 1933 but its membership numbers remained small, possibly because the Scottish communities derived, in the main, from areas where there had been no alternative to Orthodoxy. Its formation had to wait until the community was more settled and had been invigorated by the arrival of Jews from Central Europe before and after the Second World War, where Reform Judaism had been much stronger.

The Flight from Nazism

REFUGEES & THE KINDERTRANSPORT

During the 1930s refugees from Nazi Germany began arriving in Scotland. There were estimated to be around 60,000 refugees from Germany and neighbouring countries in Britain by 1939 and probably around 3,000 in Scotland. At first the arrivals were mainly German physicians who had been quickly excluded from health service practice after the Nazis came to power early in 1933. These doctors were seeking British medical qualifications and the Scottish licensing bodies offered the best opportunity to obtain the requirement for practice in Britain and Commonwealth dominions and colonies. The Scottish qualifications could be obtained after just one year of study while those in England required two or more years.

Among the early arrivals was a young doctor, Frieda Ehrlich, who had been traumatised by Nazi activity, including the placing of a bomb near her home. This emphasised the need to leave Germany and she and her husband came to Glasgow where courses for the medical refugees were quickly established in the Royal Infirmary to help them take the licensing examinations. However, it was to be some years before she felt well enough to return to her studies and achieve a place on the British Medical Register. During these years she took the initiative in finding places for refugees to come to Glasgow. In this she was helped by two key individuals, Sophie Geneen and Sir Daniel Stevenson.

Sophie Geneen, the proprietor of a kosher hotel in the Gorbals, provided affidavits for many Jewish refugees from Nazism during the 1930s by creating extra positions in her hotel. This enabled them to earn the statutory 30 shillings a week to prevent them being a charge on the country. Frieda Ehrlich met Sir Daniel Stevenson through a contact at the Glasgow Art Club. Stevenson had made a fortune as a ship broker and coal exporter and was one of Glasgow University's most generous benefactors with several chairs, a lectureship, a scholarship and a physical education building named for him. From 1934 he was Chancellor of the University and with his background in European travel and fluency in German he was deeply aware of the tragedy unfolding in Germany. Stevenson was able to use his contacts with British consuls in Germany to expedite exit visas for people known to Ehrlich. Some of those saved in this way had been detained in prison camps but there were many others who could not be helped.

Sophie Geneen dispensed charity discreetly from her kosher hotel in the Gorbals, Glasgow. She created extra positions in the hotel in the 1930s to give refugees from Nazism a fresh start.

The growing numbers of refugee physicians were welcomed to Glasgow and Edinburgh by community members. Prominent among these members was Dr Lewis Rifkind, a medical graduate of Edinburgh University who was known as a socialist and Zionist thinker and activist. His experience as a general practitioner in the mining town of Crossgates in Fife had exposed him to suffering in pit accidents and by 1930 he was working in a practice in Glasgow. He combined his professional care with a deep understanding of the predicament of the refugees and his political optimism presaged hope of a better future.

The medical newcomers were to enrich clinical and academic life in Scotland. Joseph (Joe) Schorstein (1909-1976) was the son of a rabbi in the Czech town of Brno and had graduated in medicine at the University of Vienna in 1934. He came to Manchester after graduation, trained in the developing discipline of neurosurgery and served in a neurosurgical unit during the war operating under extreme conditions at Monte Cassino. Appointed consultant neurosurgeon at Killearn Hospital, near Glasgow, after the war he developed a reputation for care and surgical excellence. He refused to carry out lobotomies for schizophrenia, calling the procedure a Nazi-like attempt to change personality, and had a jaundiced view on where technology was taking society.

Schorstein set up a study group, with lawyer-turned-psychotherapist Karl Abenheimer (1898-1973), which brought the thought and culture of Central European Jewish life through the writings of thinkers like Martin Buber to a generation of Scottish theologians, philosophers and physicians. Abenheimer published widely, both on Jewish issues and on literary analysis, and the two men had an important influence on the early life, practice and writings of the idiosyncratic Scottish psychiatrist R D Laing, at one time the best known psychiatrist in the world.

Hans Walter Kosterlitz (1903-1996) graduated in medicine in Berlin and emigrated to Scotland in 1934 where he joined the staff of Aberdeen University, at first as a research student only obtaining British qualifications in 1938. There he later served as Professor of Pharmacology and Chemistry from 1968 until 1973 when he became Director of the university's Drug Addiction Research Unit. Kosterlitz was best known for his work on endorphins and received many awards for his research. The Kosterlitz Centre at the University of Aberdeen was opened in 2010 to honour his memory.

Most of the refugee physicians who had studied in Scotland moved on to practice in England and abroad. Among those who remained in Scotland was Kate Herman (1904-2007) who obtained Scottish qualifications in 1938 and settled in Edinburgh where she was one of the first woman specialists in neuro-surgery. She trained in Edinburgh's Royal Infirmary from 1938 under one of the founding fathers of neurosurgery, Professor Norman Dott who was open to employing refugee surgeons. Colleagues paid tribute to her self-discipline and determination to stand up for what she believed in. By 1943 she was senior clinical assistant at the neurosurgical department of the Royal Infirmary of Edinburgh and also worked at the Neurological Brain Injuries Unit in the former Emergency Military Services Hospital in Bangour, West Lothian.

A number of psychiatrists, including such important figures as Willi Meyer-Gross, Erwin Stengel and Felix Post began their careers in Scotland before moving south. Some 352 refugee practitioners obtained Scottish qualifications during this period and the majority of them spent the year of preparations for the examinations in Glasgow or Edinburgh.

One of the refugee scholars who passed through Aberdeen University was David Daube (1909-1999), a graduate of the universities of Freiburg and Göttingen, widely recognised as the leading scholar of ancient law in the twentieth century, with a great expertise in Jewish and Roman law. His facility with Jewish source texts enabled him to reinterpret many New Testament passages in the light of Talmudic scholarship. Daube had arrived in England in 1933, obtaining a PhD in Cambridge in 1935. In subsequent visits back to Germany he managed to rescue relations, colleagues and friends. As Professor of Jurisprudence at the University of Aberdeen he was in Scotland from 1951 to 1955, enriching the local community with his deep attachment to Jewish study and practice. Aberdeen was a much-needed opportunity for Daube to reach professorial status and his arrival was seen locally as part of the project to create a law school of international standing in Aberdeen. Daube was then appointed Regius Professor in Civil Law at the University of Oxford, finally moving to the University of California at Berkeley, as Professor-in-Residence.

Another Jewish academic lawyer, Julius Fackenheim, was to take a leading role in the Aberdeen Jewish community serving as synagogue president for many years. Born in Halle, where he had practised as a lawyer, he arrived in Britain in 1939, settling in Aberdeen where he became Lecturer in Comparative Law and German at the Aberdeen Training College. His son, Emil, managed to join his parents in Aberdeen after being miraculously released from the Sachsenhausen concentration camp where he had been interned for three months. Emil studied briefly at the University of Aberdeen, and taught in the Aberdeen *cheder* before being interred in Britain as an enemy alien and then sent to an aliens detention camp in Quebec. In Canada he had a prominent career as rabbi and philosopher focussing on issues related to Jewish theology and the Holocaust, warning his fellow Jews against giving Hitler a posthumous victory by opting out of Judaism.

Probably the best known of the refugees are the approximately 10,000 children of the Kindertransport, mostly, though not exclusively Jewish,

Rabbi Daiches meets the first Kindertransport children to arrive in Scotland, Waverley Station, Edinburgh, 1938

Kindertransport children at music practice outside Whittingehame House, near Haddington, East Lothian.

from Germany, Austria, Poland, Czechoslovakia and Danzig, who came to Britain between Kristallnacht in November 1938 and the outbreak of war in September 1939. Organised as the Refugee Children's Movement (RCM), the process was conducted with a minimum of bureaucratic fuss. A further seven hundred children came to Britain though the efforts of Sir Nicholas Winton (1909-2015), a British stockbroker of Jewish origin working out of Prague.

One of the first hostels for the Kindertransport children, who were known as the Kinder, was the Whittingehame Farm School in East Lothian which operated between 1939 and 1941, and accommodated 160 children. Whittingehame House was the family estate, home and birthplace of the late British Prime Minister Arthur Balfour, author of the Balfour Declaration. His nephew, and heir, Viscount Traprain, conceived the idea of making Whittingehame House and its estate a centre for accommodation, education in English and Hebrew, with a two-year programme in agricultural training, which included farm management, forestry and animal nutrition. The project was supported by Youth Aliyah, a group promoting the settlement of youth in Palestine, while the children and youth leaders from the Zionist youth movements HaShomer Ha-Tzair, Habonim and Bachad (Bnei Akiva) lived and worked under one roof.

The introduction of alien internment in May and June 1940 caught Jewish refugees indiscriminately along with German Nazis who happened to have been in Britain when war began. This severely curtailed the activity of Jewish youth workers. At Whittingehame House, thirty-six older children and members of staff were removed under armed guard in May 1940 and not released for several months. The required annual running costs for the House activities were quite high and ultimately proved to be more than the communities in Glasgow and Edinburgh could raise. A new centre, which combined a Jewish and secular education with farm work, was established nearby at Polton House, Lasswade, Midlothian for about 40 teenage children. Polton House remained open after the war and accommodated some of the child survivors of

Kindertransport boys outside the hostel adjacent to the Garnethill Synagogue at 125 Hill Street

concentration camps. A further twenty Kinder were cared for at the Selkirk Priory from 1938 until 1946. Some boys were accommodated in the hostel beside the Garnethill Synagogue and a further few were admitted to the Jewish Orphanage in Glasgow.

Other Kinder were settled in foster homes around the country and some joined Jewish children from Glasgow evacuated during the war to Birkenward House in Skelmorlie and Ernespie House in Castle Douglas. Here we shall look at just some of the experiences of those who came to Scotland with the Kindertransport to give an understanding of how the children settled in Scotland and their experiences later in life.

Henry and Ingrid Wuga were both Kindertransport children and married after first meeting in the Glasgow Refugee Centre. Henry was 15 years old when he arrived in Britain and after arriving in London he came directly to Glasgow where he was first cared for by Etta Hurwich, a Jewish widow. After a few

months in Glasgow, Kircudbright and Perthshire he was interred on the Isle of Man as an enemy alien, while still only 16 years old. He had been corresponding with his family in Germany and German-occupied-France and the military censor thought he had been in

Henry and Ingrid Wuga tell their story to Scotland's First Minister Nicola Sturgeon, 2015.

contact with enemy personnel. Henry and Ingrid married in 1944 and eventually set up their own kosher catering business in Glasgow while Henry also worked as a volunteer for the British Limbless Ex-Servicemen's Association, training ex-soldiers to slalom down slopes while raising considerable sums for the charity. Only one tenth of Kindertransport children had surviving parents but Henry was fortunate that his mother survived in hiding and was able to join them in 1947. Ingrid was also 15 years old when she came on the Kindertransport. Her parents too managed to come to Britain before the War, and after a few months in England they all moved to West Kilbride where her parents found work. War restrictions on aliens living within five miles of the coastline forced them to move and this brought them to Glasgow.

Rosa Sacharin (nee Goldszal) was born in Berlin in 1925 the youngest of three children, growing up in an environment which was both very Jewish and politically very active. Her father was arrested in 1935 and the family became almost destitute overnight. Rosa was put in a children's home. Her brother was arrested after Kristallnacht and shortly afterwards she learned that she had a Kindertransport place. Located first in unsatisfactory accommodation in Edinburgh she managed to move in March 1941 to Glasgow where her sister was living, staying first in a nurses' home in Hillhead Street and then at the refugee hostel in Renfrew Street. A short spell as a teenager in a primary school gave her the language skills she needed, and after secondary school she was accepted to enter nursing at the Royal Hospital for Sick Children at Yorkhill. Rosa's mother survived the war and managed to join her daughters in Glasgow and, after obtaining a work permit, found work as a cook in Sophie Geneen's hotel. Once her mother was settled in Glasgow Rosa went to Israel in 1952 working with children at the Sarafand Hospital returning to Glasgow for family reasons. She married Joe Sacharin and gradually moved up the nursing profession to become a nursing tutor and author of nursing textbooks. In retirement she worked for many years as a volunteer with the records of the Scottish Jewish Archives Centre.

Dorrith Marianne Oppenheim (1931-2012) was born in Kassel, Germany as an only child in a family with a comfortable lifestyle. Following Kristallnacht she obtained a place on the Kindertransport never to see her parents again as they were first deported to Theresienstadt in 1943 and then the following year to Auschwitz from which they never returned. When she arrived in England, she was met by her new foster parents Fred and Sophie Gallimore at Liverpool Street Station on 26th July 1939 and went to live with them in Colinton, Edinburgh. She attended George Watson's School and was evacuated to Innerleithen during the worst part of the war. During these years she converted to Christianity although later in life she was to describe herself as a Jewish-Christian attending occasional synagogue services. She graduated in Secretarial Studies at Skerry's College in Edinburgh and on her first job she met Andrew Sim, a lawyer, whom she married after spending 18 months in Brazil, where Fred Gallimore was living.

In My Pocket

By Dorrith M. Sim

Illustrated by Gerald Fitzgerald

Dorrith Sim's book In My Pocket explains the Kindertransport for young children. Beautifully illustrated, it recalls her first words in English when all her valued possessions were in her pockets.

Dorrith and Andrew had four daughters and a son and once Andrew obtained a partnership in a law firm they settled in Prestwick where Dorrith was involved in various local organisations. After listening to a talk on Woman's Hour by Bertha Leverton, who was looking for the mainly Jewish children who had travelled unaccompanied on the Kindertransport, for the 50th anniversary reunion, she became involved with locating ex-Kinder from around Scotland, initiating SAROK in 1990, the Scottish Association of Reunion of Kinder. Her experiences encouraged Dorrith to write, and in a need to leave some sort of legacy, produced her book, especially for children *In My Pocket* in 1996. She spent many hours talking to children in schools and adults from various groups to inform them about the Holocaust and the persecution of the Jews.

Tom Berman, (1934-2013), later to become an internationally renowned aquatic scientist was brought to Glasgow as one of the children rescued from Czechoslovakia by Sir Nicholas Winton. Influenced by his involvement in the Zionist pioneering organisation, Habonim, while in Glasgow Berman emigrated to Israel in 1951 and settled in Kibbutz Amiad. He completed his higher education in the United States, first at Rutgers University followed by a PhD at the Massachusetts Institute of Technology. Besides achieving international recognition as a specialist in the study of lake ecosystems, Berman was also known for his poetry which encompassed many themes relating to his life, some from the deep emotion of his experiences on the Kindertransport while others dealt with his work on aquatic systems. Even after living in Israel for more 50 years, he still spoke with a strong Glasgow accent.

Tom Berman holding his Permission to enter Britain.

THE LEATHER SUITCASE   by Tom Berman

They don't
make suitcases
like that
any more.

Time was,
when this case
was made
solid, leather,
heavy stitching
with protective edges
at the corners.

Time was,
when voyage meant
train, steamship
distances unbridgeable
waiting for a thinning mail
weeks, then months,
then nothing

Children's train,
across the Reich
stops
and starts again...

Holland
a lighted gangplank,
night ferry to gray-misted
sea-gulled Harwich
again the rails
reaching flat across
East Anglia,
to London

in my bedroom
the suitcase,
a silent witness
with two labels

"Wilson Station, Praha"
"Royal Scot, London-Glasgow"

Leather suitcase
from a far-off country,
Czechoslovakia,
containing all the love
parents could pack
for a five year old
off on a journey
for life.

One of Scotland's leading architects of the twentieth century was Isi Metzstein, whose influential designs followed the European modernist style of Le Corbusier and the American Frank Lloyd Wright. He was responsible for some of the most remarkable and distinguished modern architecture in postwar Britain. At the Glasgow practice of Gillespie Kidd & Coia, for whom he worked throughout his career, he and his colleague Andrew MacMillan designed a series of striking churches in and around Glasgow, as well as school and university buildings further afield. They were also the architects of St Peter's Seminary at Cardross, once widely regarded as the finest modern building in Scotland but now a derelict ruin.

Metzstein was born in Berlin, the son of two Polish Jews, Efraim, who died in 1933, and Rachel. He and his siblings escaped Germany in 1939 through the Kindertransport and his mother also managed to reach Britain before the war. After being scattered around Britain the family was eventually reunited in Scotland and Isi remained in Glasgow for the rest of his life. In 1945, he left school, and he obtained an architecture apprenticeship with Jack Coia, the sole surviving partner of Gillespie Kidd & Coia. At the same time, Metzstein enrolled for evening classes in architecture at the Glasgow School of Art, where he met Andrew MacMillan, whom he brought into the firm in 1954. Together, they were to transform the practice and, as 'Andy and Isi', became a celebrated double-act, as designers, teachers and talkers.

Coia had close links with the Roman Catholic archdiocese of Glasgow, having built a number of churches in the 1930s and after War the archdiocese was about to embark on a programme of church building. Soon, the influence of Andy and Isi became evident, as they followed the European avant-garde style of buildings in continental Europe. While the Roman Catholic hierarchy believed their architect to be the legendary Coia, the designing was in fact carried out by a Jewish refugee from Berlin, who described himself as a 'lapsed atheist', and a Glaswegian of Highland Presbyterian ancestry. As Metzstein explained: that 'We were designing churches, which are one-off buildings with an emotional and religious context.' However, technical problems were to emerge with the firm's experimental buildings and Isi complained about buildings which were 'demolished or mutilated without the involvement of its designer' and which were 'the victims of brutal, premature 'scrap-heaping''.

Metzstein then devoted himself to teaching and lecturing, at the Mackintosh School of Architecture at the Glasgow School of Art, of which MacMillan was now head, and at the University of Edinburgh, where he was a professor. An obituary described him as remaining 'until the end the conscience of a rational modernity'. Metzstein's wife Danielle (Dany) was also of Central European Jewish origin and had been born in the south of France during the Nazi occupation.

During the Second World War around 900 Polish Jewish service-men were stationed in Scotland as part of the 30,000 strong Polish Army-in-Exile. Spread around the country many made contact with local communities and their religious needs were organized by the chaplain to the Polish Jewish servicemen, Rabbi Heshel Klepfisz. A major Pesach *seder*, for some hundreds of the Polish Jewish soldiers, was held in Glasgow in April 1943 when

Isi Metzstein recives an award from Princess Margaret, 1961. Photograph in Scottish Jewish Archives Centre, courtesy of Dany Metzstein.

allegations of anti-Semitism in the army were surfacing. A Jewish representative of the Polish National Council in London, Ignacy Schwarzbart, came to the *seder* taking the opportunity to meet community leaders in Glasgow who had been taking soundings about the extent of the problem. Rumblings about anti-Semitism persisted for much of the year but it was agreed that such incidents were exceptional and that the Polish Army should take action when it occurred. The concern about anti-Semitism led a number of the Jewish soldiers to desert the Polish Army for the British Army. Alarmed at the possible scale of defections a number of the Jewish soldiers in Scotland were court-martialed and sentenced by the Polish Army but soon amnestied.

Most of the soldiers were taken to Normandy to take part in the invasion of France but a number remained behind or returned to be de-mobbed in Scotland. Rabbi Klepfisz's correspondence indicates that he had the unenviable task of trying to find if any relatives of the Polish Jewish soldiers had survived in occupied France, Belgium and Holland. Klepfisz married and remained in Glasgow for a few years after the War, eventually moving on to become Chief Rabbi of Panama and an author with a special interest of the *shtetl* life in Poland in which he had been raised.

The contributions of the wartime Jewish refugees in terms of business, professions and Scottish culture were thus considerable and they formed a significant section of the Scottish Jewish community in the post-war years. There had been some tensions in the earlier years of refugee settlement between the established

community, of Eastern European origin, and the Central European newcomers. In the post-war era such distinctions were of no importance.

Lyn Wolfson's Holocaust Memorial at the Cathcart Hebrew Cemetery, Glasgow: The Star of David (Magen David) is shattered into six pieces which together with the six pebble represents the six million murdered by the Nazis and their allies. This follows the custom to place a stone when visiting the grave to honour the memory of the decease and to affirm that 'you are not forgotten'. (Courtesy: Lyn Wolfson)

Migration from Scotland

1900–1945

In considering Jewish migration around the turn of the twentieth century we have noted that Glasgow was not seen widely as the place of final destination. Most Jews from Eastern Europe were heading for the United States, and especially New York. Scotland was often seen as a staging post, a convenient stop on the way west, a place to learn English and to make a start in adapting to western ways. If success came then one could stay, if not the option of further travel could be taken up. The First World War does mark something of a watershed, with immigration dropping to negligible levels. There had been anecdotes of significant onward migration of Jews resident in Scotland, but without British nationality, in the 1920s. However, this study has indicated that such numbers were comparatively small.

During the years of Jewish mass migration from east to west there were many stories of travellers being robbed, tricked or

Re-enactment of Jews arriving in Glasgow to mark 150 years of continuous Jewish welfare in the city by Jewish Care Scotland, 1858-2008.

duped by unscrupulous characters at the various stations and ports on the migrant routes. Most concerning was the presence of human traffickers in what was known as the 'white slave trade' with ruthless traders selling women into prostitution in such port cities as Shanghai and Buenos Aires. At first the Glasgow Jewish community supported the efforts of the Scottish National Vigilance Association but in 1913 they agreed to fund a worker at the port to ensure travellers' safety.

Glasgow featured as one of the Jewish 'port cities' in *Jews and Port Cities 1590-1990*, edited by David Cesarani and Gemma Romain. Glasgow attracted immigrants both as an important port on the Jewish transmigration route and as a growing commercial and industrial central. For Jews the city offered a safe haven in terms of a low level of anti-Semitism given the preoccupation of the majority Protestant population with the large Irish Catholic immigrant community.

Early in the nineteenth century the Ashenheim brothers, whose parents had come to Edinburgh from Holland, both qualified in medicine and emigrated to begin their medical practice. Louis Ashenheim, the first Scottish born Jew to graduate at a Scottish university obtained the MD degree from the University of St. Andrews in 1839, though he had studied in Edinburgh, and settled in Jamaica in 1843. He was active there not just as a doctor but also as a journalist and freemason, and his descendants were leading members of the Jewish community and prominent in local politics. His younger brother Charles had long and interrupted undergraduate studies in Edinburgh but eventually graduated there in 1852 and settled in the newly established town of Dubbo in New South Wales.

One of the families spending some time in Glasgow before earning enough money for the next stage of the journey from Lithuania to New York was that of Harris Morris Kaplan. Like Elimelech Berislasvky, whose story is told in Chapter 5, Kaplan seems to have been sold a ticket from Lithuania directly to Glasgow. Kaplan, a furrier's son from Shavli in Lithuania, anglicised his surname to Copeland while living for a few years in Glasgow, and his youngest child Aaron, born in Brooklyn in 1900, was to achieve considerable musical fame as Aaron Copeland. One of Copeland's earliest musical interests was with klezmer and synagogue music. He had a long and distinguished career as a composer and later as a conductor. His left-wing politics put him on an FBI list of communist sympathisers in the 1950s.

Another migrant to the United States of America was Abram Belskie (1907-1988) who was brought to Glasgow at the age of two by his parents who had moved from Poland to Britain settling first in London. Belskie's father was a tailor and the family remained in deep poverty, unable to provide drawing materials for the young Abram, who showed artistic talent at an early age. With the help of various scholarships, including the John Keppie Travelling Scholarship in 1926, and winning the Sir John Edward Burnett Prize in 1928, he was able to study at the Glasgow School of Art from 1926 and even to have a tour of Continental Europe to see developments in art there. Returning to Glasgow he set up his own studio but soon felt constricted by the art scene in Glasgow and set sail for New York in 1929.

In 1931 he moved to Closter, New Jersey where he became a stone carver later specialising in medical illustration, creating realistic medical models and later producing a series of fifty medical medallions. His work won many awards in America and in 1993 the Belskie Museum of Arts and Science was opened in Closter to preserve, house and exhibit his works.

Besides onward migration to North America, records indicate Jews from Scotland settling further afield. Often this was related to Jews with qualifications, especially in medicine, where finding employment in Scotland was difficult given the large size of the medical schools. Chaim Bermant once remarked that almost all of the Jewish students he had been friendly with at Glasgow University in the 1950s had left the city, mostly going to London and the 2001 Census indicated that over 2,000 Scottish born Jews were living in England.

Hyam Goodman, whose father was the *shammas*, collector, at Garnethill Synagogue, received the significant bursary of £100 for his MA degree before he undertook medical studies gaining further bursary funds of £300. He was the first Jewish President of the Glasgow University Students' Representative Council, graduating in 1897, and settling in South Africa after working as a surgical resident in Glasgow's Western Infirmary.

Southern Africa was a popular choice for onward movement from Glasgow. Rabbi Isaac Zwebner came to Glasgow, from his native Jerusalem, with his wife Rella, to study at the University of Glasgow around 1937. During the years they spent in the community Rabbi Zwebner set up a Hebrew speaking circle, taught in the *cheder*, Hebrew classes, in Falkirk, led services in the Ayr Synagogue during the High Holy Days and served as Headmaster of the Giffnock Synagogue Hebrew Classes until leaving Glasgow in 1943. In 1953 Rabbi Zwebner took a post in South Africa moving to Rhodesia in 1967. Nine years later in 1976 the Zwebners returned to Israel leaving their community in Bulawayo, where Rabbi Zwebner had served as Chief Rabbi of Rhodesia.

While the bulk of *aliyah*, migration to Israel, took place following the establishment of the State in 1948, movement to Palestine by Jews from Glasgow began in Ottoman times. We have already noted that the first rabbi in the Gorbals, Abraham Shyne, had settled in Jerusalem after the death of his wife around 1907. In 1909 the Glasgow Agudas Olei Zion, Glasgow Group for Ascent to Zion, was established to facilitate the founding of a co-operative farming development in the Galilee. Several families enrolled, saving enough funds, around £6 a year, to begin their new lives. The scheme was unique in the western world and Dr Franz Oppenheimer, the force behind economic and agricultural components of Zionist settlement, paid a visit to Glasgow from

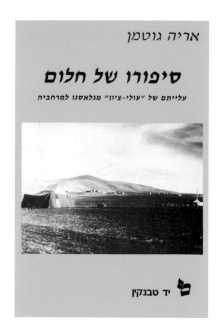

Berlin to review progress. The new arrivals found the work to be hard, the climate far from congenial, accommodation basic and they were prone to disease. While some families returned, disillusioned, to Glasgow other, like the Gutmans were more successful. Shmaryahu Gutman, was born in Glasgow in 1909 and brought to Palestine by his parents in 1912. He became an archaeologist and is credited with the promotion of Masada as a rallying point for the Zionist endeavour taking generations of Jewish youth there from around 1936.

Isaac Michaelson was born in 1903 in Edinburgh and graduated in medicine there in 1927. He studied Ophthalmology at the University of Glasgow and the University of Edinburgh and worked as a pathologist at the Glasgow Eye Infirmary and served as a lecturer at the University of Glasgow. During World War II, he was an advisor to the British Army on ophthalmology and served in Egypt with frequent visits to Palestine. In 1948, he completed his doctorate and emigrated with his family to Israel. However, his interest in *aliya* dates back to April 1930, when, having just completed his basic specialist training, he applied to Dr Avraham Ticho, then the leading ophthalmologist in Jerusalem, for a position as his assistant. Ticho was unable to offer Michaelson a job at the time. However, in a nice turn of events Michaelson established a series of memorial lectures in 1970 to honour the memory of Dr Ticho. In 1954, he became Director of the Department of Ophthalmology at Hadassah University Hospital in Jerusalem and was also appointed as a Professor at the Medical School of the Hebrew University of Jerusalem. Much of Michaelson's work was to assist developing countries, particularly in Africa, in developing ophthalmic services and preventing blindness. He was awarded the Israel Prize, in medicine, in 1960.

Professor Isaac Michaelson, Glasgow graduate and Professor of Ophthalmology at the Hebrew University-Hadassah Medical School. He was awarded the Israel Prize for Medicine in 1960. He is photographed here with Dr Avraham Ticho, for long the leading ophthalmologist in Israel.

A number of Scottish Jews also moved back to various places in Western and Central Europe during the 1920s and 1930s. Some of them managed to return to Scotland before the outbreak of War and others had harrowing tales of survival in Nazi occupied Europe. Fifteen Scottish born Jews, mostly from Glasgow, are listed in the victims of the Holocaust in the Hall of Names at Yad Vashem and survivors include Jews from Scotland who were the subjects of the notorious Nazi medical experiments.

Jews also returned to Russia from Scotland. While the London Jewish Board of Guardians organised large scale repatriation to Eastern Europe, numbering possibly as many as 50,000 Jews, of those they thought unlikely to settle successfully. The Glasgow Board was responsible only for returning those who wished to do so, usually for family or religious reasons. However, a number of Jews did return to Russia for ideological reasons. Glasgow Jews could be numbered amongst the Conventionists, a group of soldiers recruited after the British Army introduced conscription in 1917. Jews without British nationality, who were a considerable proportion of the community, had the option of joining the British Army or returning to fight with the Russians. The Convention was agreed by British and Russian Government in July 1917 after the fall of the Tsar and there was hope of a new more democratic country emerging.

Nathan Katzanell was one of the Glasgow Jews who signed up for the Russian Army and the local Jewish welfare bodies undertook to help support families whose breadwinners had joined up. By the time he reached the Russian port of Murmansk the country was in turmoil on the eve of the Bolshevik Revolution. The situation at the port was described as 'primitive and chaotic' and Katzanell decided to head south on his own not trusting the train that was provided. He spent the next two years travelling through Russia and the Ukraine, through territory racked by civil war and anti-Jewish pogroms, finally reaching Odessa where he boarded a ship heading for Britain. He was fortunate to be able to smuggle himself on shore at Swansea as returning soldiers had no right of re-entry and indeed only one third of the Conventionists made it back.

Ralph Glasser recounted the tale of the Varnett family who returned to Soviet Russia from Glasgow in 1924 in his book *Growing up in the Gorbals,* believing the propaganda of a 'workers' paradise, and was never heard of again. Glasgow born Flora Leipman was taken to the Soviet Union by her mother and step-father in 1933, when she was 14 years old. Her mother was arrested as a spy and incarcerated in the Gulag and Flora was imprisoned for several years in the notorious Dolinka Camp in Kazakhstan. It took the personal intervention of Sir Geoffrey Howe, then British Foreign Secretary, to obtain her release and return to Britain in 1984, and to a reunion with her brother who had miraculously escaped from the gulag and made his way through Siberia eventually reaching America.

Flora Leipman. The illustration on the left shows her as a child on holiday in Dunoon in 1929 while on the right we see her with local children at Chukota in the Urals in 1963, after release from labour camps.

9

Jews and the Arts

Jewish involvement in the cultural life of Scotland dates back to the era of mass immigration during the nineteenth century, but subsequent migrations through the twentieth century have also enriched the arts in the country. This chapter looks at the contribution, and the legacy, providing an overview of just some of the artists who settled, or were sheltered, in Scotland. Some of these personalities were immigrants while others reflect a later stage of community life.

One example of this involvement in Jewish communal life in Glasgow is Michael Simons (1842-1925) who arrived in Glasgow with his parents from London when only three years old. His father Benjamin set up and ran a successful fruit business which was based in

Michael Simons in the robes of a Glasgow Bailie. He was a businessman, arts patron and community leader as well as a Justice of the Peace and Deputy Lieutenant for the City of Glasgow.

Glasgow's Candleriggs and became one of the largest fruit brokers in the world with offices in the USA and Canada. Simons was elected to the Glasgow City Council in 1883, the first Jew to become a Glasgow councillor, even before any members of the much larger Catholic community had been elected. He was involved in just about every aspect of Glasgow's Jewish communal life, always ready to speak on a wide range of his subjects and his recognition as a prominent citizen, involved in civic and cultural matters, did much for the acceptance of the Jewish community as an integral part of the life of the city.

He convened a number of committees associated with the great Glasgow Exhibitions of 1890 and 1901 and was offered, but, declined, the position of Lord Provost. He did, however, serve as a Justice of the Peace and Deputy-Lieutenant for the city of Glasgow and was appointed a Bailie. Simons used his position to advance the role of culture in the lives of the city's working classes and he was for a time Chairman of the Royal Glasgow Institute of Fine Arts. In 1895 Simons founded the Howard and Wyndham theatre group becoming director and chairman, formalizing the arrangement whereby the two impresarios ran the Royal Lyceum Theatre in Edinburgh. The company expanded to take in the Theatre Royal and King's Theatre in Glasgow as well as others in Dundee, Aberdeen and locations in the north of England.

Benno Schotz (1891-1984) was born in Arensburg, Estonia and came to Glasgow in 1912 to study at the Royal Technical College, receiving an engineering diploma in 1914. For the next nine years he worked in the drawing office of John Brown, Clydebank shipbuilders, while attending evening classes at the Glasgow School of Art. He was appointed Head of Sculpture at the Art School in 1938, a post he held till his retirement. In 1963 he was appointed the Queen's Sculptor-in-Ordinary for Scotland and he became a Glasgow City Freeman in 1981. His pupils included a refugee student from Berlin Inge (Neufeld) King and Hannah Frank (1908-2008). Under Schotz's guidance Hannah Frank's early black and white drawings gave way to sculptures in plaster, terra

cotta or bronze. Schotz provided practical support, including sponsorships and exhibitions, for the wartime refugee artists in Glasgow, including Josef Herman (1911-2000) and Jankel Adler (1885-1949). A committed

Benno Schotz models Arie Leib Jaffe, Zionist leader and chief editor of Haaretz. He was director-general of Keren Hayesod until March 11, 1948, when he and 12 others were killed by a car bomb in the courtyard of the Jewish Agency building in Jerusalem.

Hannah Frank:
'Chanukkah', from
Glasgow Talmud Torah
brochure 1949

Zionist, Schotz sculpted heads of Herzl, Ben Gurion and Golda Meir and his work can be found in galleries around Britain and Israel. The Kelvingrove Art Gallery and Museum has a significant collection of his work. His sculpture *The Psalmist* can be seen in Kelvingrove Park and other examples of his work can be found in a number of Glasgow churches.

Schotz's legacy is easy to identify through his years as a teacher of sculpture at the Glasgow School of Art. Adler and Herman can also be considered as having had an influence on Scottish art, despite their few years in the country, through their participation in the founding of the New Scottish Group under its President J D Fergusson.

Other significant Glasgow Jewish artists during this period included Louis Freeman (1891-1972), David Hillman (1894-1974) and Joseph Ancill (1896-1949). Freeman was known professionally as Scottie Wilson and he is considered a leading example of twentieth century outsider art, developing a personal code of morality in his art where evil characters are set beside symbols of good. Hillman was the Russian born son of Rabbi Samuel Hillman, and his studies at the Glasgow School of Art, where he was the first Jewish graduate, brought about a rift between the artistic son and the traditionalist rabbi. Hillman excelled in synagogue stained glass window art and their richness of colour, delight in the Jewish festivals and his mastery of the Jewish sources can be seen in many synagogues in London and at the Hechal Shlomo Jewish Heritage Centre in Jerusalem. Ancill was a student at the Glasgow School of Art where his

David Hillman's stained glass window depicts the imagery of the Pesach (Passover) Festival. The window shows the table set for the seder (family meal with the retelling of the story of the Exodus from Egypt), with matza (unleavened bread), wine and the ritual seder plate. (Courtesy, Heichal Shlomo, Jewish Heritage Centre, Jerusalem and Daniel Pearlman, 2D Photography)

Jewish contemporaries included Saul Yaffie and Amy Esterson. Ancill was best known for his portraits of community leaders such as Sir Maurice Bloch and Benjamin Strump. He was also commissioned to paint the portrait of Glasgow Lord Provost James Welsh at the end of his term of office in 1945.

Two of a series of drawings reflecting pre-war Jewish Warsaw by Josef Herman during his years in Glasgow, 1940-1943. These 'Glasgow Drawings' illustrate many different aspects of life in the teeming Jewish neighbourhoods of pre-War Warsaw. In these drawings we see examples of Jewish working men.

As we have seen, the dislocations of the 1930s and the Holocaust era brought such well-known artists as Josef Herman and Jankel Adler to Glasgow for a few years. Herman used his time in Glasgow to create an art series known as the Glasgow Drawings in which, as he explained:

I was drawn to depict all I could remember (of traditional Jewish life in Warsaw) as faithfully as a chronicler, though always in colours and scenes that expressed my own nostalgia for a vanishing past and a deep sense of sympathy for the millions of Jews who had remained in Eastern Europe and who were being systematically starved, humiliated and extinguished ... I walked the streets of the Scottish city and all I could see was what my memory wanted me to see, a fabric of distant life, which was nonetheless part of me.

Adler held a one man show at the Annan Gallery at Charing Cross in 1942 and worked with Herman and other local artists in designing sets for the Unity Players, a theatre group with a left-wing ethos, in which Avrom Greenbaum's Jewish Institute Players often had a leading role. His major work *Two Rabbis* was created while he was in Glasgow.

Refugees from the Holocaust who settled in Glasgow include the sculptor Paul Zunterstein (1921-1968), artist and designer Hilda Goldwag (1912-2008) and Marianne Grant (1921-2007). Zunterstein arrived in Glasgow in 1938 and began art studies at the Glasgow School of Art subsequently teaching there and exhibiting regularly at the Royal Glasgow Institute of the Fine Arts and at the Royal Scottish Academy. Hilda Goldwag, a graduate of the Viennese Graphische Lehr und Versuchsanstalt left Vienna to settle in Glasgow in March 1939, but permits for her family to join her arrived only as war began and they all perished. Goldwag worked as a commercial designer and illustrator and from the 1950s she resumed painting and exhibiting. Her painful memories of her family never left her and her creative output bears testimony to her deep personal pain as much to her strength of intellect, her spirit and he trained artistic talents.

Marianne Grant was born in Prague and was a survivor of Terezin, Auschwitz and of the 'death marches' being finally liberated by the British Army at Bergen Belsen. In the concentration camps she drew what she saw around her whenever she could get artistic material. After the War she was taken to Sweden as part of a Red Cross initiative and she came to Glasgow in 1951 after marrying, in London, the Rev Jack Grant, Headmaster of the Queens Park Synagogue Hebrew Classes and later Minister of the Newton Mearns Synagogue. Her Holocaust art was eventually purchased by the Glasgow Museums and some of her paintings are on display at the Kelvingrove Art Gallery and Museum. A major exhibition of her art work was staged in 2002 with an accompanying booklet *I Knew I Was Painting for my Life*.

'I knew I was painting for my life' Marianne Grant's Holocaust art work, Kelvingrove Art Gallery and Museum.

In more recent times, Jewish artists in Glasgow have included the sculptor Lyn Wolfson (1946-) and Alma Wolfson (1942-), who has exhibited widely and is renowned for her portraiture of Scottish landscapes.

Within the field of literature, we have already had recourse to *Two Worlds: An Edinburgh Jewish Childhood* by David Daiches, son of Rabbi Dr Salis Daiches. Daiches (1912-2005) had further reflections on his childhood and Jewish life in Edinburgh in *Was: A Pastime of Time Past*, a book full of literary wit and style. Besides his own creative literature, he made his mark as a teacher, critic, historian and scholar. After many years in academic posts in America he became professor of English (1961-1977) and Dean of the School of English Studies (1961-68) at Sussex University. From 1980 to 1986 he was director of the Institute for Advanced Studies in the Humanities at Edinburgh University (1980-86) spending his last years in the city he always regarded as home. He was recognised as one of the most prolific and respected academics of his time with works on a variety of topics, from Scotch whisky and the Scottish Enlightenment to *Moses: the Man and His Vision.* His sister Sylvia Daiches Raphael was a distinguished linguist, translating Balzac's works into English. She was in Glasgow from 1949 to 1972 during which time her husband David Daiches Raphael was Professor of Political and Social Philosophy at the University of Glasgow. Later, in London she was Warden at the (independent Reform) Westminster Synagogue

David Daiches' daughter, Jenni Calder was herself an acclaimed author who had a lengthy career in a number of key posts at the National Museum of Scotland. In her autobiographical work *Not Nebuchadnezzar* she explored her inherited Jewish and Scottish roots. Though born in America, Calder clearly felt that Edinburgh was home in the way that no other place could be and the legacy of her rabbinic grandfather and her mother's Scottish farming roots led to an identity which moved beyond her father's *Two Worlds* though she was clearly influenced by it. Closely affected by anti-Semitism and troubled by the Israel-Palestinian conflict, her identity came to be formed by what she was not rather than something more positive, hence the title of her personal memoir.

Avivah Gottlieb Zornberg, who grew up in Glasgow, was the daughter of Rabbi Dr Wolf Gottlieb, rabbi of the Queens Park Synagogue and Av, head, of the Glasgow Beth Din, religious court. Zornberg began her career as a teacher of Bible around 1980 and has published several books, beginning with *Genesis: The Beginning of Desire in 1995.* Further books, including *The Particulars of Rapture: Reflections on Exodus and The Murmuring Deep: Reflections on the Biblical Unconscious,* display her understanding of psychoanalytic resonance, finding layers of meaning within the plain reading of the text, while using midrashic commentaries to reveal deeper and more complex levels of interpretation. These are works of great intellectual achievement showing how Zornberg has created a unique role for herself as a teacher of Bible.

The towering figure expressing the Jews and Scots in Glasgow was undoubtedly Chaim Bermant (1929-1998). Born in Latvia he was brought to Glasgow in 1937 where his father, a rabbi and *shochet,* had found employment. Bermant wrote extensively about his experience of childhood and adolescence in Scotland. He was educated at Queen's Park Secondary and his first degree, in Economics, was at the University of Glasgow. Growing up in a religious home and blessed with an enquiring and liberal mind Bermant was able to point to the foibles and misdemeanours of those in authority while expressing a love for the different aspects of his identity.

As a journalist, writing for the *Jewish Chronicle,* his comment column gave him a well-deserved national reputation, but his memoir *Coming Home*

The Patriarch

A Jewish family saga by

Chaim Bermant

Dust jacket of Chaim Bermant's major multi-generational novel of Jewish immigrant life, The Patriarch, as the Lithuanian Rabinovitches settle to Jewish life in Scotland as the Raeburn family. The cover illustration is by Judy Bermant.

and several of his novels display an accurate, and sometimes biting, insight to what made up Jewish life in Glasgow in the 1950s, when the community was at its peak. In his first novel *Jericho Sleep Alone* we have the coming of age story of a Jewish boy in Glasgow with many of the supporting characters thinly disguised parodies of community members. *Ben Preserve Us* describes the happenings of a penny pinching synagogue in the fictitious Scottish town of Auchenbother as they discover that their young rabbi has received a large inheritance. Two other novels also feature Jewish Glasgow. *The Second Mrs Whitberg* describes the last Jewish inhabitants of the decaying Gorbals. His major work, *The Patriarch* is a true Jewish family saga which follows the life and family of Nahum Rabinovitz from the *shtetl* of Volkovysk to Glasgow, where he prospers and changes his name to the more Scottish Raeburn, and sees his next generation spread out around the world. Nahum's experiences, in novel form, illustrate many of the themes of migration, displacement, integration and material success, and the description of the first generation, physically in Glasgow but emotionally still in the *shtetl*, forms the heart of many works on the modern Jewish story.

Jews were also represented in the popular music halls of Glasgow.[1] The so-called Hebrew comedians, inspired by trends in the American music hall, pandered to anti-Jewish prejudices with their racial stereotyping. They portrayed an unflattering appearance of the immigrant Jew, with his distinctive clothing, appearance and accent which clearly bordered on the anti-Semitic. Two Glasgow Jewish comedians, Blass and Spilg, performed on the stage as Peel and Curtis but the master of the Jewish music hall genre was

---

[1]   I would like to express my thanks for this information to Paul Maloney, taken from Chapter 4, 'Ikey Granitesteen from Aberdeen': Jewish Stage Representations in Glasgow Music Halls, of his forthcoming book *Britannia Panopticon Music Hall and Cosmopolitan Entertainment Culture*, Palgrave MacMillan, 2016.

Ike Freedman (1895-1960). Ike grew up in the Gorbals and while his talent took him to England and America, he was clearly a product of Jewish Glasgow. The Yiddish theatre, catering exclusively to Jewish audiences, remained popular in Glasgow until the 1930s, both with drama and such music hall songs as *Ich bin a Bocher fun di Gorbals!* (I am a Young Man from the Gorbals).

A more positive image of the Jewish immigrant appeared in the frequent staging in Glasgow of the Jewish-American drama *Potash and Perlmutter* set in the New York rag trade. In time, Glasgow's Jewish community came to embrace music hall, as seen in the success of the Frutin family who became leading purveyors of Scottish variety and pantomime, and also through its own social activities, which by the 1920s included variety performances alongside traditional entertainment.

The leading Jewish theatre group in Scotland, the Glasgow Jewish Institute Players, was first formed in 1936 by Avrom Greenbaum (1903-1963), and based at the Bloch Little Theatre at the Jewish Institute in South Portland Street. Greenbaum was born in Izbica, a small town of a few thousand inhabitants in the Lublin region, whose population was almost entirely Jewish. He was brought to Glasgow when just a year old, growing up in a traditional Jewish family and working as a tailor, though his first foray into amateur theatre began as early as 1923. In his stage work, both as a writer and director, he examined aspects of the human condition, Jewish oppression in Europe and the rights of mankind. These themes were examined in such plays such as *The Bread of Affliction*, which looked at Russian persecution of the Jews

Scene from The Dybbuk by S. Ansky performed in 1951 by the Glasgow Jewish Institute Players at the Bloch Little Theatre, Gorbals, Glasgow. The play tells the story of the possession of a young woman by a dybbuk, a malicious spirit, of her dead beloved.

and was published in a book of leading plays in 1937-8. The following year his play *Ecce Homo* provided what has been described as an 'ironic indictment' of Christian persecution of the Jews. In 1941 the company formed the left-inclined Glasgow Unity Theatre group, with the Glasgow Workers' Theatre Group, the Clarion Players and Glasgow Corporation Transport Players.

Greenbaum also enjoyed dabbling in poetry, combining traditional Scottish expressions with Yiddish ones. His *Address to the Fress* was a parody of Burns' *Ode To a Haggis*.

> *Lives there a man sae thrawn and frugal*
> *Wad turn up his neb at lockshen kugel?*

Burn's disparaging of religious hypocrisy in Holy Willie becomes a comment on those people Greenbaum saw in his own community whom he felt were overly concerned with religious minutiae, describing them, in a mixture of Scots and Yiddish, the *unco-froom*:

> *O, gie me the man wha isna blate*
> *When self-appointed machers rant,*
> *Tae tell them they maun gang their gate*
> *Or, aiblins, Schlog zich kop'n vant.*

After the war the Jewish Players left the Glasgow Unity and concentrated on presenting their own productions. Popular playwrights included Clifford Odets, Philadelphia-born son of Jewish immigrants, and a founding member of a highly influential New York theatre company that utilised an acting technique based on that of the Russian director Constantin Stanislavski. For the Glasgow Jewish Arts Festival of 1951 the Players staged a memorable performance of Anksi's *The Dybbuk*, symbolising artistic and Jewish roots but staged within a Glasgow milieu, rather than the original setting of the Ukraine. Avrom Greenbaum died in 1963 and as a tribute to his memory, those remaining in the company re-styled themselves as the Avrom Greenbaum Players.

Jewish theatre in Glasgow was also associated with Cecil Taylor (1929-1981), who was known professionally as C P Taylor. He was born in Glasgow, the son of immigrant parents, with politically radical views and strong ties to the Labour Party. His plays often had Glasgow Jewish or more widely Jewish themes, often infused with a socialist outlook. Of his eighty plays he is best remembered for the frequently performed *Bread and Butter* and *Good*. *Bread and Butter* follows two Jewish couples from the 1930s Gorbals to the 1960s Queens Park as they live their simple lives against the backdrop of momentous events not too far from home. *Good* was first staged by the Royal Shakespeare Theatre and tells the story of a liberal German academic who becomes involved in Nazi war crimes while still seeing himself as a good man.

In television and the media Glasgow can claim both Sir Jeremy Isaacs and Stephen Morrison. Isaacs (born 1932) grew up in Hillhead, the son of a jeweller and a GP, and was educated at Glasgow Academy and Merton College, Oxford. He joined Granada Television as a producer in 1958, creating or supervising major series, becoming Director of Programmes for Thames Television in the 1970s. Isaacs also worked for the BBC and later became the first Chief Executive of Channel 4 setting its innovative style in a mix of high-brow and more populist programmes. After leaving Channel 4 he became General Director of the Royal Opera House, Covent Garden and between 1997 and 2000 he was President of the Royal Television Society. Isaacs was Patron of Glasgow Jewish Arts in 1990, a major festival organised as the Jewish participation in Glasgow's year as European City of Culture. In a Foreword to its *Jewish Arts Anthology* he described how his Jewish upbringing in Glasgow, and the city's artistic and cultural treasures showed him that 'the value of the artist lasted longer and meant more...than material success.' He first experienced music at St. Andrew's Hall, theatre at the King's and James Bridie's plays at the Citizen's and recalled the high standards of the Glasgow Jewish Institute Players, describing them as 'very nearly the best amateur dramatic society in Britain in their day'.

Stephen (Steve) Morrison (born 1947) grew up in Glasgow where his father and his older brother, ran a Jewish delicatessen. He studied Politics at the University of Edinburgh and in 1968, he became the first student to stand for the post of University Rector. After attending the National Film and Television School, he was a radio producer with BBC Scotland before joining Granada Television in 1974 becoming Director of Programmes and, in 2001, Chief Executive. He was elected Rector of the University of Edinburgh in 2015.

One of the dilemmas a study like this faces is over questions of definition, status and identity. Jews are traditionally defined as born of a Jewish mother or converted by a recognised religious authority. Muriel Spark (1918-2006) undoubtedly had a Jewish background. She was born in Edinburgh, the daughter of Bernard Camberg, an engineer, and Sarah Elizabeth Maud (née Uezzell). Her father was Jewish and she always claimed that her mother had been raised a Presbyterian, though it seems that her parents had a Jewish wedding, which could only have followed her mother's religious conversion. Spark was educated at James Gillespie's School for Girls and the family lived in the Bruntsfield area of Edinburgh. In 1937 she married Sidney Oswald Spark, and followed him to Southern Rhodesia (now Zimbabwe) where their son Robin was born in July 1938. In 1940 Muriel left Sidney and Robin returned to Britain with his father later to be brought up by his maternal grandparents in Scotland.

Spark began writing seriously after the war, under her married name, beginning with poetry and literary criticism. In 1954 she decided to join the Roman Catholic Church, which she considered crucial in her development toward becoming a novelist. In 1963 she described in fictional form what is was to be half Jewish in her story *The Gentile Jewesses*, and later developed the theme in her novel *The Mandelbaum Gate*, which won the James Tait Black Memorial Prize, and the *Yorkshire Post* Book of the Year 1966. Though she

Robin Halevy Spark, oil painting on canvas illustrating the Succot festival. Reproduced from the Tenth Anniversary Magazine of the Scottish Jewish Archives Centre (1997) which appeared with the kind permission of the artist.

wrote more than twenty novels, she is probably best remembered for *The Prime of Miss Jean Brodie* (1961) based on her old school in Edinburgh and published to much critical acclaim.

She was completely estranged from her son Samuel Robin Spark, who followed a Jewish way of life and was fully accepted as a member of the Edinburgh Hebrew Congregation. This, in effect, confirmed his grandmother's Jewish conversion, an event that Muriel would never acknowledge though she did admit that her mother had taken part in a Jewish wedding ceremony. Robin Spark took up art work late in his career and produced many hundreds of works, covering a wide range of themes, and in particular touching Jewish religious topics. His art has been widely exhibited.

Moving further from the Jewish community we have Marion Bernstein, daughter of a Jewish immigrant father from Germany and an Anglican mother from London, who settled in Glasgow in 1874. Living in Glasgow's Paisley Road she was noted as observing the Sabbath on Saturday, which may reflect Seventh Day Adventist practice as well as a nod to her Jewish ancestry. Two years later she published a collection of a hundred poems, with the title *Mirren's Musings*. This collection included some radical feminist writings, tackling such themes as the living and working conditions of the urban poor and the role of women in society. These poems established her reputation and they are still being studied actively today. A collection of her works, entitled *A Song of Glasgow Town*, was published in 2013.

Jews in Business

10

As we have seen Jews were first attracted to Scotland, and Glasgow in particular, for the economic opportunities available in the expanding Victorian city. Glasgow and Dundee benefitted from the arrival of Jewish textile agents who had commercial links with companies in Hamburg. Outside the main cities were such businesses as Finkelstein the jewellers in Inverness, the Bernstein furniture store in Dunfermline and a series of kosher hotels and guest houses in Ayr. It was one of these, the Invercloy Hotel, which housed the synagogue of the Ayr Hebrew Congregation.

It would not be possible to give a comprehensive picture of Jewish involvement in business in Scotland. The following few businesses have been included as they illustrate some of the immigrant themes covered in the study. The immigration from Eastern Europe at the end of the nineteenth century and the beginning of twentieth brought a new generation of whose first steps at financial independence often began as pedlars or credit drapers. There were many businesses set

Business premises of the jewellery shop of Finkelstein, Inverness

up during these years all over Scotland. Some of these were to falter and fail but others retained the family feel and a few developed into substantial companies.

Immigrant Businesses

Typical of these family immigrant enterprises is the furniture business established by Louis Taylor in Falkirk. Taylor had been born in the small village of Klikol (Klykoliai) in northern Lithuania in 1884 but had been brought to the Jewish neighbourhood of South Terrace, Cork by his parents at the age of two years. The Cork Jews, like many in Glasgow, had significant family links to Klikol and the neighbouring *shtetls* like Zhogger (Zagare) and Akmeyan (Akmeniai). Moving first to Glasgow he was already settled in Falkirk by the 1911 Census, when he was lodging with Sophia and Max Spilg, son of the community's minister. Described in the Census as a 'traveller and general dealer' he was selling goods in the neighbouring mining towns until he was able to set up his own furniture store in town by 1921. He was to be joined in business by his son Harold, who was born in Falkirk, and at the time of writing (2016) the business was still operating successfully in Manor Street, in the Falkirk town centre, with Raymond, and his son Lawrence, the third and fourth generations of the family in the business. Taylor's was not the only Jewish furniture shop in Falkirk as there had been others run by the Riffkins, and Cembler and Marks families.

Howard Denton, born Hyman Zoltie in Edinburgh just before the First World War, was the son of Maurice Zoltie, one of three brothers who had run a tobacco business in Bialystok. Maurice Zoltie began his working life in Scotland as one of the *trebblers,* the Yiddish speaking pedlars who travelled from Edinburgh to the Fife mining towns with their backpacks selling a variety of household goods. Though personally observant Maurice and his wife did not manage to pass their style of Eastern European piety to their children. Although Denton strayed from his parents' Judaism his upbringing in the warm atmosphere of Edinburgh's immigrant neighbourhood, affectionately called the 'Happy Land', produced a lifelong attachment to his Jewish background.

Denton was taken out of school to work in a tailoring workshop at the age of fourteen. Following a short period of army service at the beginning of the Second World War Denton worked first as a photographer before his entrepreneurial instincts led him into a number of pursuits, most of which were successful. A spell in sales in America convinced him to return to Edinburgh where his photographic company achieved some success for a time. Finally, it was as a restaurateur that he was to make his mark, first in partnership but then opening his own chain of self-service restaurants in the 1960s, called the Farmhouse, which specialised in organic products. His life story was published in 1991 and was broadcast on Radio Scotland.

Another small business of the immigrant period was the blacksmith workshop established by David (Tuviya) Tobias who had come to Scotland from Ostrolenka (Ostrołęka) a town north east of Warsaw, in May 1886 crossing the

North Sea from Hamburg to Leith. The ship's manifest indicated he was travelling without his family, though accompanied by some others from Ostrolenka. Tobias had married in 1881 and he sent for his family once he was settled in Glasgow, also being joined by his father Harris, aged around 60 years, who must have been one of the older immigrants amongst the predominantly young community.

David (Tuvia) Tobias and son Osher at the smithy, around 1930.

Strictly observant, Tobias struggled to find work where he could observe the Sabbath and where he could stop weekday morning work at daybreak to recite the daily prayers. He was to set up his own smithy, initially situated in the quaintly named Schipka Pass, which ran under the railways viaduct between Gallowgate and London Road, but no longer exists. The smithy would be closed on Saturdays and Jewish festivals, a policy continued by his sons after his death.

Tobias had a traditional religious education. Ostrolenka had a cheder which was supplemented by a Talmud Torah and a yeshiva. In Glasgow he participated in Talmudic learning groups, the Chevra Shas, within the small Poalei Tzedek Synagogue in the Gorbals, and had a teaching session of a folio page, *blatt* or *daf*, of the Talmud with his grandsons on a Saturday afternoon. Photographs of him in the smithy always show him wearing a large black yarmulke typical of religious Jews.

Goldbergs

Abraham Goldberg came to Scotland from Dublin around 1908. He had married Bessy Margolis in Dublin in 1905 and their oldest son Ephraim was born there in 1907. In Glasgow he began dealing in bales of cloth. His first shop opened in the Gorbals soon after his arrival in the city and this was to grow over the years into a network of over a hundred stores. The business moved to Glasgow's Candleriggs in the 1920s and this remained the site of the main department store for almost seventy years. The Candleriggs store was closed on Saturday from the beginning though as other stores opened they followed regular Scottish retail hours. In 1934 Abraham Goldberg handed over the running of the company to his sons Ephraim and Michael (Melech) and within a few years the company was quoted on the Stock Market.

The Goldberg family were devoted members of the Jewish community, and Ephraim and Michael were prominent as activists in its welfare and educational organisations, besides being major philanthropists. Michael Goldberg was also involved in the cultural life of the city and was for many years Chairman of the Citizens' Theatre. He encouraged a wider repertoire of plays, and was the key figure behind the development of the Close Theatre where more experimental plays, including CP Taylor's *Bread and Butter*, were performed.

Bread and Butter, C P Taylor's play of two Jewish couples in Glasgow with their aspirations and views of religion, socialism and Zionism from the 1930s to the 1950s remains popular with theatre-goers.

In the post-war period the company expanded rapidly and could claim a number of significant innovations. A major store was opened in 1965 in the Tollcross neighbourhood of Edinburgh. Its distinctive architecture and in-store facilities, including a crèche, proved to be extremely popular in its early years and it too remained closed on Saturdays, at least initially. Community bloggers still reminisce about the flagship stores with one describing it as 'my fantasy store ... there will never be another one like it'. Department stores, but much smaller than the one in Candleriggs, opened in various Scottish towns including Falkirk, Ayr, Dunfermline and Greenock and the growing new town of East Kilbride. In 1974 Mark Goldberg, grandson of the company's founder, became company chairman and a new era of expansion and innovation followed. Mark followed his father and uncle into Jewish community activity, and became involved in various Glasgow Jewish organisations and was Chairman of the Glasgow Jewish Community Trust, of which his father and uncle were founder members. The Community Trust disbursed major sums to Jewish cultural, welfare and religious charities in the city.

Goldbergs pioneered an electronic point of sales system, credited with enabling IBM retail software to enter the European market, replacing the paper record keeping which was both expensive to maintain and slow to operate. In 1979 a chain of fashion stores, aimed at a younger market, opened under the brand name of Wrygges, and the company also owned the Schuh and Ted Baker stores. In 1984 the company produced its own credit card. It had always provided easy purchase terms on extended credit for its goods but the addition of the Style credit card enabled it to offer credit in a more modern way. The card proved popular and was eventually purchased by the Royal Bank of Scotland. However, the 1980s proved to be challenging times for the retail market. Financial problems in the wider economy and the growth of competition, in the crowded British retail environment, affected sales and eventually pushed the company into losses which forced its closure in 1990.

Sir Isaac Wolfson

Probably the best known Jewish businessman to emerge from Scotland is Sir Isaac Wolfson (1897-1991), son of Solomon and Necha Sarah Wolfson, who left Rajgród, a small mostly Jewish, village about thirty miles from Bialystok in Poland, to settle in the Gorbals. Wolfson was born in Glasgow and was educated at Queen's Park School, Glasgow where he excelled in mathematics but, as he could not afford to train as an accountant he became a salesman for his father, who was a cabinet maker, earning 5 shillings a week at the age of 14 years. Chaim Bermant remarked that Wolfson read 'balance sheets like other people read thrillers and he can weave through the most complicated accounts like a Cabalist through the intricacies of the Zohar'. His father is said to have recognised him

Sir Isaac Wolfson: Glasgow born businessman philanthropist and community leader

as a financial genius by the age of 9 years and, encouraged by his sales successes in Glasgow, he left for London in 1920 where he married Edith Specterman in 1926. Her father owned a chain of cinemas and was helpful in Wolfson's early career. Wolfson joined Great Universal Stores (GUS) in 1931 and within three years he was Managing Director. Displaying outstanding financial acumen, began a programme of expansion and aggressive acquisitions which increased the value of the company twenty-fold by the end of the War. By the 1970s the company owned more than 2,000 stores besides having the largest mail-order business in the country.

One of Wolfson's acquisitions, in 1957, was the extensive stores network, with over 400 branches, established by Max and Edith Morrison, who had been married in Libau, Latvia around 1890. Edith Morrison had been trained in dress-making by the Court Dressmaker in Reval, Estonia before coming first to London, and eventually after a few years there, to Glasgow. Despite bringing up seven children Edith managed to be both a mother and a business woman. The business began with a sewing workshop in Abbotsford Place soon moving along the road to South Portland Street, in the heart of the Gorbals. The business, under the leadership of the next generation, gradually moved from manufacturing into retail and the transition was complete by 1935. With financial success, Edith's sons Hyam, Peter and Jack became major philanthropists endowing major projects in Britain and Israel.

Wolfson maintained the religious orthodoxy of his childhood and when he became President of the United Synagogue in 1962. He was the first President to be descended from the wave of nineteenth century Jewish immigrants and the first to be personally observant. He supported many charities, Jewish, Israeli and numerous academic and medical bodies across Britain. Colleges were named after him at both Oxford and Cambridge. His Wolfson Foundation had disbursed £20 million pounds by 1970 and £130 million by the time of his death. He funded the Chief Rabbinate building in Jerusalem, Hechal Shlomo, named for his father. He received a baronetcy in the Queen's 1962 New Year's Honours list and the following year was elected a Fellow of the Royal Society. In recognition of his philanthropy in Glasgow he was awarded the Freedom of the City of Glasgow in 1971. He died in Israel, where he maintained a home in Rehovot, in 1991, aged 93.

Scotch Whisky

A few Glasgow Jews were involved in the whisky trade, including the Heilbrons in the nineteenth century and Samuel (Rosenbloom) Campbell and Sir Maurice Bloch (1883-1964) in the twentieth century. Bloch, the son of Elias and Zippe Leah who were married in 1878 in Zagare, was born in Lithuania, and his brother Joseph was born in Scotland. The two brothers showed an early interest in whisky distilling, leaving Dundee in 1910 for Glasgow where they set up Bloch Brothers (Distillers) Ltd. Maurice was quickly involved in Jewish community activities, especially the Queen's Park Synagogue, the Glasgow Jewish Board of Guardians and the Glasgow Jewish Representative Council, when it was founded in January 1914. He was already prominent and supportive enough to be asked to perform the opening of the new synagogue in his home town of Dundee in 1920. By then he was involved in negotiations with the Scottish Office about providing training for Jewish school leavers and was instrumental in helping to set up an endowment fund for the Jewish Board of Guardians, of which he was later Chairman. Active in Conservative and Unionist politics he stood unsuccessfully for Parliament three times for the Gorbals constituency from 1929 to 1935 but does not seem to have had enough support from the Jewish voters, who tended to vote for the Labour candidate, to change the outcome of the elections. As Representative Council President from 1936 to 1940 he showed great skill in protecting the Jewish community from threats from fascist elements and religious extremists. His political and social services work was recognised by the award of a knighthood in 1937.

Ambassador – the flagship whisky of Bloch Brothers (Distillers) Ltd. A well-regarded blend of classic malt whiskies.

Bloch Brothers (Distillers) Ltd. purchased the troubled Glen Scotia Distillery in Campbeltown in 1930 and a few years later, in 1941, it acquired the Scapa Distillery in the Orkneys, possibly to provide the Scapa malt whisky for the Bloch's premium Ambassador blend. The Ambassador Blend, matured for 12 or 25 years, became one of the few blends that enjoyed the patronage of malt whisky enthusiasts. Bloch sold the company in 1954 to Hiram Walker to devote himself to philanthropic activities supporting medical bodies in Scotland and giving generously to charities within the Jewish community and in Israel. In 1956 he set up the Maurice Bloch Trust, a charitable foundation for the advancement of the Jewish religion and education and for the cure and alleviation of sickness and disease. The Trust's first sizeable gift was to the University of Glasgow, to endow an annual lecture on some aspect of medical science or practice. There is a Maurice Bloch Lecture Theatre at the Royal College of Physicians and Surgeons of Glasgow. The Bloch Trust remains today, more than fifty years after his death, a major source of funding within the Glasgow Jewish community, now managed, like the Winocour Trust, by the Glasgow Jewish Community Trust.

Refugee Businesses

One of the businesses established by a Jewish refugee from Nazism was Kid-Knit established by Willi Goldschmidt after fleeing from Nazi Germany. Adapting the patterns and designs from his German factory in his children's clothing factory in the east end of Glasgow he produced high quality clothes for shops throughout Britain. Kalman (Charles) Frischer was born in Krakow, but moved to Germany, where he married Helene Altwein in Leipzig in 1932. Before his marriage, Kalman was an amateur boxer with the Bar Kochba sports club in Leipzig, where he later had a fur factory. In 1938, the Frischers, and

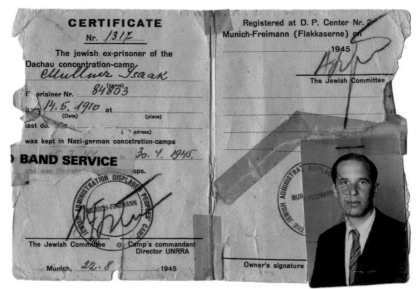

CERTIFICATE
Nr. *1317*

Registered at D. P. Center Nr. 2
Munich-Freimann (Flakkaserne) on
.... 1945

The jewish ex-prisoner of the
Dachau concentration-camp

Müllner Isaak
(name)

The Jewish Committee

Prisiner Nr. *84803*

born *14.5.1910* at
(Date)   (place)

last do..............(adress)

was kept in Nazi-german concetration-camps

BAND SERVICE

30. 4. 1945

and was liberated............ops.

The Jewish Committee   Camp's commandant
Director UNRRA

Munich, *22. 8*............ 1945

Owner's signature

Isaak Millner, a native of Kovno (Kaunas) and survivor of Dachau came to Glasgow after the war, where his wife had family, with his wife and daughter and established a knitwear business. His wife, Haja (Chaya), survived the notorious Stuttholf Camp and a forced (death) march as the Germans retreated, while their daughter Golda had been smuggled out of the ghetto and was sheltered by a farming couple. Golda married Joe Frischer, whose family had managed to reach Glasgow before the war.

their children Joe and Evelyn, were deported to Poland as they did not hold German nationality. They managed to emigrate to London, then Glasgow, where Kalman re-established his fur business.

Another such business was Textile Engineering founded in 1951 by Jack Tiefenbrun (1920-1985). Jack had been born in Krakow, Poland, and the family moved to a farm outside Vienna when he was five years old. He arrived in the UK in 1938 and his first job involved maintaining large knitting looms and at the same time he completed a part-time engineering qualification at college. By the age of thirty he had the wealth of engineering knowledge and experience needed to start his own company. The Textile Engineering Company serviced a wide range of customers while dealing mainly with the Singer Sewing Machine Company at Clydebank. In 1963, the company moved from a former snooker hall in the Gorbals to a purpose built factory in the south side of Glasgow and was renamed Castle Precision Engineering Ltd. In recent years, with Jack's son Marcus (1954-2014) as Managing Director from 1993 the company became a leading British sub-contractor for precision components for the aerospace, defence, energy and electronics industries. Yan Tiefenbrun, Marcus' son and the third generation in the company, joined Castle in 2007.

Jack's older son Ivor, who was born in the Gorbals, is the founder and Chairman of Linn Products Ltd, Glasgow-based manufacturers of hi-fi audio equipment and home theatre equipment. He began his work experience at Castle Precision and started Linn Products in Glasgow's Castlemilk in 1972 to manufacture a hi-fi turntable, which would produce the best possible musical sound, creating the Linn Sondek LP12, which was a market leader for three decades. With the assistance of his father he succeeded in manufacturing a turntable which would not be adversely affected by the loudspeakers, proving that designing a better turntable was the key to better sound. The system was even built to cope with adaptations as technological improvements became available and the company remained able to adapt to the rapid changes in the industry.

Honours quickly flowed. He was awarded the MBE in 1992 for services to the Electronic Industry and received the Scottish Entrepreneur of the Year Award in 2001. Ivor, a popular and often controversial speaker, was well known as a supporter of the Conservative Party and especially of its long-time leader, Margaret Thatcher, who was widely reviled in Scotland. His son, Gilad, joined the business in 2003 as Research and Development manager moving up to Managing Director in 2009 with Ivor becoming Executive Chairman.

11 Jews in the Professions

There is probably no other field where the Jewish contribution to Scotland has been as profound as in the professional sphere. Fuelled by a desire to rise above the ghetto trades of the first generation and encouraged by families and an open society which encouraged learning, Jews moved quickly into professional life. We have noted that the first professionals in the Jewish community were the various rabbis and ministers who were employed by the various Scottish synagogues. Here we mention just a few professionals whose careers illustrate aspects of the Scottish story.

Some of the early Glasgow Jewish community were opticians. David Davis, who had arrived in Glasgow around 1823, and served for many years as President of the fledgling Jewish community was described in the Post Office Directories, as an optical and mathematical instrument maker, with premises at 98 Trongate. Members of the family had been in London at the end of the eighteenth century and they gradually expanded their optician businesses to several cities around Britain with David's brother, John Isaac Davis, establishing himself in Edinburgh. The Davis family changed over to selling jewellery and silver. Another early Jewish optician in Scotland was Isaac Lazarus, (1810-1879). He began working in the early 1830s, initially for John Isaac Davis in Edinburgh. In the mid-1840s he changed his name to John Lizars and he set up the J Lizars Company in Glasgow in the 1850s.

Medicine

From the middle of the nineteenth century Jewish students living in Glasgow and Edinburgh began to graduate in medicine. These include the Ashenheim brother, Louis (1839) and Charles (1852) in Edinburgh, who migrated to practise in Jamaica and Australia respectively, and Asher Asher

Asher Asher, physician and community worker.

(1856) and Samuel Levenston (1859) in Glasgow. Asher worked in Glasgow and Bishopbriggs for a few years before leaving for London where he initially worked in a Jewish practice in London's East End before becoming the first Secretary of the United Synagogue when it was formed in 1870. Levenston was, as we have noted, a member of the family of medical botanists, and was eventually struck off by the General Medical Council for alleged irregularities in his practice.

That medicine was an early and popular choice for the first Jewish students in Scotland is confirmed by the high proportion of medical graduates especially among the children of Jewish immigrants. By the 1930s Jewish medical undergraduates considerably outnumbered all the other Jewish students. The law profession was seen as unwelcoming to Jews and places in legal firms hard to obtain. Moreover, medicine was seen as having a higher social status than some other options such as teaching. This move into medicine was a worldwide Jewish phenomenon. The numbers of Jews wishing to enter the medical profession sparked the introduction of a quota system in some of the more prestigious American medical schools. Quota systems had existed from Tsarist times in Russian medical schools leading to Jewish students taking degrees in places like Switzerland or France. From the late 1920s American Jewish medical students were studying in significant numbers in Edinburgh and Glasgow, joined by Jewish students from South Africa where medical education was in its infancy.

On the other hand, the Scottish medical schools were big enough and the Jewish community small enough for all the local Jewish students who wished to enter medicine to find a place to study. Even before the First World War around twenty Scottish Jews had graduated in medicine though just a handful remained to practise in Scotland. Scottish medical schools trained far more doctors than could be accommodated in the country and a high proportion moved south to England or went overseas. During the 1920s there were more than eighty Jewish medical graduates and by the 1930s there were more Glasgow Jews studying medicine than from the larger communities of Manchester and Leeds. In fact, more remarkably, the number of Edinburgh Jews was not far behind that for Manchester and Leeds with around a fifth of the Edinburgh cohort group in medical studies.

An examination of the addresses on the matriculation slips of Jewish medical students in Glasgow, who attended classes between 1895 and 1945, shows that around two thirds lived in the immigrant area of the Gorbals or the Battlefield district to its south, popular with the next generation. About a quarter came from homes in Glasgow's West End. Parental occupation details on these slips show that Jewish students were twice as likely to have artisan fathers as the student body as a whole with more in small businesses and less than half with a professional father.

One of the best known Edinburgh general medical practices was that of the Lipetz brothers Julius (1903-1972) and Samuel (1897-1983). Julius (Julie), joined his brother Sam's practice in the Pleasance after graduation in 1926, a poverty stricken area with overcrowding, insanitary conditions, rat infestation, and high unemployment. Julius became a lecturer at the Department of General Practice of the University of Edinburgh after wartime service in Africa and Italy. Sam, like many Jewish practitioners of his generation, continued working into old age not retiring until the age of 85. He was awarded an MD in 1947 for his work on peptic ulcer and was active in the Socialist Medical Association, remaining an active member of the Communist Party. He described himself as an agnostic who had pride in his Jewish background and showed a deep concern for social justice. He was once almost mugged by a gang in the Canongate, while out on a night call to a patient, until a voice called out, 'Don't bash him. It's the wee doctor!'

Jewish practitioners could be found in the smaller Jewish communities too. Maurice, son of Isaac Finkelstein who was both a noted philanthropist, jeweller and community leader in Inverness, graduated in medicine in the University of Edinburgh, as Dr Finlayson, continuing to work as a pathologist in Edinburgh until awarded a Rockefeller Fellowship to work in America. He subsequently emigrated to South Africa where he started a family wine business at Hartenberg Farm in Stellenbosch, which has continued into the third generation and is credited with bringing modern winemaking to the Cape region.

The Dundee Jewish community benefitted from the presence of Dr David Jacob and his son Albert who were prominent figures for many decades. David, who came from a poor background, managed to complete his studies with numerous scholarships and grants. He graduated at the University of St Andrews with honours and returned to Dundee where he practiced and was active in the community. His son Albert, an academic general practitioner, was awarded an MD in 1962 and a master's degree in medical science in 1982 for work on the pattern of medical care in a new health centre. He was to gain

Dr Albert Jacob's memoirs deal with his life in the Jewish community in Dundee and the tumultuous events in which he was involved during the 1980s.

national attention when he led opposition to the decision of the Labour-led Dundee City Council to twin with Nablus, as a gesture of solidarity with the Palestine Liberation Organisation. This move prompted widespread disquiet in the wider British Jewish community and at the same time there was some opportunistic anti-Semitic activity by the far right. Albert Jacob made aliya to Israel in 1991 working as a family doctor for five years in Beersheva.

The first Jewish doctor in Glasgow to be appointed to a Regius Chair in Medicine was Noah Morris (1893-1947)[1]. Morris was the son of Henry and Sarah Gersuny from Riga and Vilna respectively, and it is said that they took their surname from the captain of their ship on the crossing to Scotland. At Glasgow University he graduated with a BSc, with special distinction, in physiology in 1913, following that with an MB ChB, with commendation in 1915, and an MD with honours in 1921, when he won the Bellahouston Gold Medal. He became a fellow of the Royal College of Physicians and Surgeons of Glasgow in 1921. During the First World War he served in France and Italy as a captain in the Royal Army Medical Corps before returning to Glasgow where he was appointed professor of physiology at the Anderson College of Medicine, Glasgow, in 1920. During this time, he also worked as a general practitioner, when he was known to leave money for medicines in the poverty-stricken homes of his patients. This experience influenced his outlook and clinical teaching in later years.

Noah Morris, the first Jew in Scotland to be appointed to a university Regius Chair.

Morris' outstanding career had a profound impact on the generations of students and physicians he taught as well as the patients who benefitted from his medical innovations. He was appointed to the post of university lecturer in paediatric biochemistry in 1928 forming a powerful research team, which published widely. He established the first diabetic clinic in Glasgow and received the prestigious degree of DSc from the University of Glasgow in 1934. Morris was appointed, in 1937, to the Regius chair of Materia Medica and Therapeutics, based at Stobhill Hospital, and the appointment was widely celebrated in the community. Despite his enthusiasm for laboratory science he warned of the dangers of unquestioning belief that a biochemical

1   Biography details from British Geriatric Society Archives, by John C Brocklehurst 26/2/2013

report solves the problem, and reminded his students that the patient is a human being with all the desires, hopes, emotions, and fears of humanity.

Morris was profoundly affected all his life by his Jewish education and background and played an active part in the Glasgow Jewish community, particularly in the field of education. In the 1930s he helped many refugee doctors who had come to Glasgow to requalify after leaving Germany or Austria and in 1939 the family received a boy who had arrived in Britain through the Kindertransport. Noah Morris was a man of great erudition balanced by humanity and approachability and his reputation as a teacher rested not only on his medical expertise but also on his vivacity, his enthusiasm, and his provocativeness. It was his firm conviction that 'the teacher had failed in his intentions if at the end of his discourse he was not mentally exhilarated and physically exhausted'.

Regarded as one of the outstanding medical scientists of his generation Abraham Goldberg (1923-2007) grew up in Edinburgh winning the Crichton Scholarship to study medicine at the University of Edinburgh, where he later obtained an MD, with the Bellahouston Gold Medal, for his thesis on porphyria, a rare but important disease affecting the carriage of oxygen in the blood. After post-war army service he worked in London in chemical pathology and then in haematology in Salt Lake City before being invited to become a lecture in Clinical Medicine at the University of Glasgow. His outstanding research on porphyria and lead poisoning was followed in 1967 by his appointment to a personal University chair in medicine, subsequently succeeding to the Regius Chair of Materia Medica where Noah Morris had excelled a generation before.

He became chairman of the clinical research board of the Medical Research Council in 1973 and five years later was appointed to the Regius Chair of the Practice of Medicine at the University of Glasgow. His expertise and encyclopaedic knowledge led to other honours. He was Chairman of the Committee on the Safety of Medicines and was founder President of the Faculty of Pharmaceutical Medicine of the UK's Royal Colleges of Physicians. He was knighted in 1983 for his services to

Professor Sir Abraham Goldberg who grew up in Edinburgh and whose work at the University of Glasgow confirmed his status as one of the leading medical scientists of the time.

medicine. It was said that his genius lay in observing what people had seen and drawing inferences that no-one else could. In his retirement he was a Research Fellow with professorial status in the Department of Modern History at the University of Glasgow giving lectures to Jewish organisations on topics which included Herzl and Freud.

Other leading Jewish medical figures in Glasgow included the general practitioner Dr Jack E Miller (1918-2008) who was Treasurer of the British Medical Association for many years, President of the Glasgow Jewish Representative Council and a founding member of the Scottish Jewish Archives Centre. He was involved in countless other areas of medical and community activity, including marriage guidance, kosher school meals, Soviet Jewry and the Glasgow Association of Jewish Ex-Servicemen of which he was Chairman for many years.

The surgeon Henry Tankel (1926-2010) was, like Jack Miller, a President of the Glasgow Jewish Representative Council and involved in a myriad of medical and Jewish organisations and activities. He was a first aider as a teenager during the Clydeside Blitz and commanded a medical reception centre in Malaya and Singapore during national service from 1949 to 1951. He received a Fulbright Scholarship to Mount Sinai Hospital in New York from 1954 to 1955 and trained as a surgeon at the Western Infirmary in Glasgow. Tankel was appointed a consultant surgeon at Glasgow's Southern General Hospital in 1962, a post he retained until retiring in 1991. His dedicated interfaith work, especially his leadership of a religious dialogue with the Church of Scotland, led to his being the first Jew to address the Church's General Assembly. Both Miller and Tankel were awarded the OBE for their services to medicine and to the community.

Lawyers

In the legal profession, as we have noted, Jewish lawyers only reached significant numbers after the Second World War. One of the best known Jewish legal figures was Lionel Daiches QC (1911-1999), the older son of Rabbi Dr Salis Daiches. From his student days he was recognised as an outstanding speaker, witty and eloquent, and his progress, interrupted only by wartime service in North Africa and Italy, including the beachhead at Anzio, led to service as a Sheriff in Glasgow. However, it was as a QC defending clients in the High Court that built his reputation as being able to speak spontaneously and appropriately with wit and style.

In the post-war era no fewer than four Scottish Jews have served in the High Court. The first was Lord Manuel Abraham Kissen, (originally Kissenisky) (1912-1981) who had been born in Vilna and was a graduate of the University of Glasgow with both an MA and LlB. After the Second World War he was admitted to the Faculty of Advocates and held a number of positions as a legal adviser to government departments and was chairman of the Law Reform Committee for Scotland. He was appointed a Senator of the College of Justice in 1963, becoming Scotland's first Jewish High Court judge.

Isaac Philip Caplan (1929-2008) was born in Glasgow and studied law at the University of Glasgow. His parents came to Glasgow as children, his father having been born in Bransk and his mother in Odessa. Before promotion to the High Court in 1989 he had been Sheriff of Lothian and Borders and subsequently Sheriff Principal of North Lanarkshire. He was judge in the legal action following the 1988 Piper Alpha disaster which took over three years in court. Philip Caplan was an enthusiastic and serious amateur photographer and a Fellow of the Royal Photographic Society.

Isaac Philip Caplan (1929-2008) was Sheriff of Lothian and Borders and then Sheriff Principal of North Lanarkshire before elevation to the High Court in 1989.

Sir Gerald Gordon, described as one of the most influential figures in Scottish criminal law and procedure in the last century, was born in 1929, studied at Glasgow University and became an advocate in 1953. In the 1960s he was a procurator fiscal in Edinburgh leaving the service to head a new department at Edinburgh University eventually becoming Dean of the Faculty of Law. He held a personal chair in law from 1969 and was appointed to the chair of Scots Law in 1972. In 1976 he moved to Glasgow serving first as Sheriff in Hamilton and then in Glasgow being appointed as a temporary judge to the Court of Session and the High Court of Justiciary from 1992 to 2004. A master of legal reasoning he was famous for 'his short charges to juries, saying in five minutes what takes many judges half an hour or more'. His work *The Criminal Law of Scotland* is regarded as the leading source on Scots criminal law both by the courts, where it is referred to frequently, and by law academics. He is the editor of *Scottish Criminal Case Reports* and of *Renton and Brown's Criminal Procedure*. He was knighted in 1999, having previously been made a CBE, and was elected an Honorary Fellow of the Royal Society of Edinburgh in 2002, the only lawyer to hold this distinction.

Hazel Cosgrove (née Aronson), was born in Glasgow in 1946 and graduated in law at the University of Glasgow in 1966. In 1968, she was admitted to the Faculty of Advocates and was the first female Sheriff of Glasgow and Strathkelvin, from 1979 to 1983, and Sheriff of Lothian and Borders from 1983 to 1996. As Lady Hazel Cosgrove she became the first woman to be appointed to a permanent seat as a judge in the Court of Session in July 1996. In February 2003, she was appointed to the Inner House of the Court of Session, composed of the ten most senior judges in Scotland who make up the Appeal Court in criminal and civil cases. She has served as chair of both the Mental Welfare Commission and the Expert Panel on Sex Offending and her report on sexual crimes in Scotland led to the establishment of the National Sex Crimes Unit. She received a CBE in 2004 for services to the criminal justice system in Scotland.

Parliamentarians and Diplomats

Scotland has also had a few Jewish MPs. The first was Emanuel (Manny) Shinwell (1885-1986) who was born in London. His family moved to Glasgow where his father opened a small clothing shop. He began his working life as a machinist in a clothing workshop and in 1903 he joined the Amalgamated Union of Clothing Operatives, and was a union delegate to the Glasgow Trades Council in 1906. He played a prominent role in the six-week Glasgow seamen's strike which began in 1911 and became active in seamen's unions. In 1919, he was involved in clashes between police and protesters in George Square and was tried for incitement to riot and sentenced to five months' imprisonment.

He was elected MP for Linlithgowshire for the Independent Labour Party in 1922 and after losing his seat in 1924 was re-elected at a by-election in 1928. From 1930 Shinwell served as Secretary for Mines but he again lost his seat in 1931 and when he returned to Parliament in 1935 it was for a seat in County Durham. In 1938 during a debate in the House of Commons he slapped the face of a Conservative MP responding to what he took to be an anti-Semitic remark after being told to 'go back to Poland'. After the Labour victory in 1945 he was Minister of Fuel and Power, and he presided over the nationalisation of the mining industry. He subsequently served as Secretary of State for War and then Minister of Defence. He was elevated to the peerage as Baron Shinwell of Easington in County Durham in 1970. He continued to be active in the House of Lords until shortly before his death.

Michael Marcus, from Edinburgh, was one of the two Dundee MPs elected in 1929, serving as Parliamentary Private Secretary to the Under-Secretary of State for Scotland. He failed to be elected in 1931 when the seat was won by a Liberal. Myer Galpern was elected the first, and so far the only, Jewish Lord Provost in Glasgow, in 1958. He was MP for Glasgow Shettleston from 1959 to 1979 and was a Deputy Speaker of the House of Commons from 1974 to 1979. He was knighted in 1960 and was given a life peerage as Baron Galpern of Shettleston in 1979.

Maurice Miller, (1920-2001) was a general practitioner, who identi-fied with the left-wing of the Labour Party and entered Parliament in 1964 after serving as a Glasgow City Councillor since 1950. He was first MP for Glasgow Kelvingrove, transferring to East Kilbride in 1974 after boundary changes. He was a strong campaigner for religious and racial tolerance and a staunch sup-porter of the State of Israel. He became the honorary parliamentary doctor providing medical advice for many of his colleagues.

Sir Malcolm Rifkind, KCMG, QC, (b.1946) is the Scottish Jewish politi-cian with the longest service in Government, reaching the position of Foreign Secretary (1995-1997) having previously been Secretary of State for Scotland

(1986–1990) and Defence Secretary (1992–1995). As Foreign Secretary, Rifkind committed the British Government, for the first time, to a Palestinian State on the West Bank and in Gaza. He entered Parliament as MP for Edinburgh Pentlands from 1974 and held the seat until 1997. He returned to Parliament in 2010 as MP for the Kensington and Chelsea seat and was appointed chairman of the Intelligence and Security Committee, having previously been Chairman of the Standards and Privileges Committee of the House of Commons.

Rifkind's family had settled in Edinburgh by 1901 with the arrival of his grandparents Charles (Chatzie/Yehezkel) Rifkind and his wife Nechama Pessil Hoffenberg from Maishad (Mosedis) in Lithuania. Charles and his brother Motte (Max) were two of the *trebblers* described by David Daiches in *Two Worlds*, selling drapery on credit round the small Fife mining communities. Charles was a very observant member of the Edinburgh Hebrew Congregation leading both its Talmudic study and High Holy Days prayers. His son, Elky (Eliyahu) Malcolm's father continued the business, selling furniture, clothing as well as drapery and was also a much respected member of Edinburgh's Jewish community. Rifkind's rise to the highest political positions in Britain, and recognised as a 'Tory grandee', one of the Conservative Party's most experienced senior figures, indicated the public acceptance of Jews at every level of society.

Sir Horace Phillips KCMG was born in Glasgow in 1917, the oldest son of a tailor brought to Glasgow as part of a group of Jewish tailors recruited to work for a Glasgow firm in 1874. He began work after school as an Inland Revenue clerk, as the family did not have the resources for him to study at university but following wartime army service, where he reached the rank of major, he entered the Diplomatic Service, serving first as Vice-Consul in Shiraz, in Iran. He was appointed British Ambassador to Saudi Arabia in 1968 but the Saudis vetoed his appointment when they discovered, thanks to an article in the *Jewish Chronicle*, that he was Jewish with a membership of Garnethill Synagogue which he maintained until his death in 2004. He had major diplomatic postings in the 1970s, notably as High Commissioner in Tanzania and Ambassador to Turkey.

A more unusual diplomatic career was that of Neville (Mandel) Lamdan, who was born in Glasgow in 1938, son of a Russian-born immigrant. After an MA at Glasgow University, he gained a DPhil at Oxford University for a seminal study of 'The Arabs and Zionism before World War I'. In 1965 he joined the British Foreign Office as one of the first Jews to be accepted on a direct entry, following a Royal Commission's recommendation that the Foreign Office's intake be representative of Britain. He served at the British Embassy in Tel Aviv (1967-1971) but then returned to Oxford intent on an academic career. In 1973, however, he accepted a temporary contract at the Israeli Foreign Ministry, which evolved into a distinguished 30-year career as an Israeli diplomat. He held many key posts relating to Egypt, Lebanon and the Peace Process, eventually serving as Israel's ambassador to the United Nations in Geneva and to the Vatican, where Pope John Paul II made him a Papal Knight in 2002.

Scotland's Jewish Communities

IN CHANGING TIMES

The figures of births and deaths generated by the study indicate that the Jewish population in Scotland reached its peak during the 1930s and that numbers remained stable until a steady decline, slow and imperceptible at first, began around 1960. At the same time the small Jewish communities around the country gradually disappeared as a better educated generation moved to Glasgow or Edinburgh or even further afield, mainly to England, Australia, North America or Israel. The last Jewish birth in Inverness was recorded in 1958, by which time the community had ceased to exist. Greenock's last Jewish birth was just a few years later. The communities in Dunfermline and Falkirk lasted at least until after the end of the Second World War. *The Jewish Chronicle* noted, in March 1950, that the Falkirk Hebrew Congregation's *Sefer Torah* had been donated to a synagogue in Israel. Although these communities had been dissolved, a nucleus of families or individuals, especially those tied to family businesses, could often still be found there.

The Ayr community survived a bit longer. It had had a revival during the War as families from Glasgow moved from the city, the site of heavy German bombing. During the 1950s the very active community was clearly declining in numbers as its members returned to Glasgow. The synagogue building was closed and a new synagogue constructed in the kosher Invercloy Hotel in 1956. This stabilised the situation for some years but by the 1970s the Ayr community was at an end.

The communities in Aberdeen and Dundee have proved to be more resilient. Their survival was helped by having synagogue premises which functioned also as a meeting place for holiday meals and social get-togethers. Yet, these two communities have survived when many much larger communities in England, such as Sunderland and Blackpool have been disbanded. The Aberdeen Synagogue, based in a granite terraced house has four floors providing space for the caretaker, the synagogue, the meeting rooms and an attic flat which has provided much needed income. While numbers dropped steadily from the 1950s there remained a nucleus of members prepared to maintain traditional services into the 1960s and 1970s. When it became difficult to maintain a regular minyan, Shabbat services were held just a couple of times a month as well as on Jewish holidays. Aberdeen has kept a policy, to this day, of keeping the synagogue doors open every Friday evening throughout the year, never knowing how many people might turn up.

Left: Interior of the Dundee Synagogue, built for the community by the Dundee City Council after the original synagogue was demolished in a slum clearance. The blue tiling and double ark, where the Torah scrolls are housed, suggests that the city architect, unfamiliar with European synagogues, modelled his designs on the style of oriental synagogues. Right: The entrance to the Meadow Street Synagogue, Dundee with Hebrew inscription over the doorway. (Courtesy Dundee City Archives)

Both Aberdeen and Dundee have been innovative in finding ways of keeping the Jews in Grampian and Fife involved in some way in their activities and their continued existence has been bolstered by the activities of the Scottish Council of Jewish Communities (ScoJeC). The Council has held events throughout Scotland from the Borders to the Highlands and Islands bringing together the scattered individuals whether in the small clusters in Aberdeen and Dundee or those loosely associated with the Jewish Network in the Highlands. New methods of communication and contact and regular social events have created a sense of belonging to the Jews identified on the twenty-first century Censuses as living in remote rural areas.

Chanukah 2006: Jews from around the western Highlands gather in Lochgilphead to kindle the Chanukah lights commemorating the victory of the Maccabees over the Seleucid Empire and the rededication of the Temple in Jerusalem in 164BCE.

The larger communities have also been affected by numerical decline. By the 1980s the Edinburgh Synagogue downsized by selling the community centre and dividing the synagogue into two areas, creating a new events area on the ground floor with the services held upstairs. In recent years, synagogue membership has continued to decline although the Edinburgh area still has around a thousand Jews, who self-identify in the Censuses though not necessarily seeing membership of an Orthodox synagogue as a priority. Edinburgh still maintains a lively journal, the *Edinburgh Star*, and an active Jewish Literary Society, founded in 1888, which brings an array of national figures to the city. It now also has a small Liberal community, *Sukkat Shalom*, as well as a Chabad House, where religious and social activities are held.

The figures indicate that the Glasgow community was at its peak from the 1950s until the mid-1960s. Jews were moving southwards from the 1930s and 1940s from Langside and Queens Park creating new communities in Clarkston and Giffnock. A community further south in Newton Mearns was established in the 1950s. In this period of growth and expansion the new Giffnock and Newlands Synagogue, with more than 1200 seats opened in 1969. The Synagogue complex housed all the associated usual religious and social facilities, including a new *mikva*, and indicated a sense of solidity, permanence and indeed announced its presence as the leading synagogue in the community.

John K Clark's windows were originally designed for the Queens Park Synagogue in Glasgow. When this synagogue closed the windows were transferred to the Giffnock and Newlands Synagogue in 2002. This window illustrates the festival of Simchat Torah, Rejoicing of the Torah, which celebrates the completing of the annual cycle of Torah readings.

At the time Glasgow Jewry was torn apart by a bitter rivalry between Rev Dr Cosgrove of Garnethill Synagogue and Rabbi Dr Wolf Gottlieb, rabbi of the Queens Park Synagogue, an accomplished scholar and orator and Glasgow's *Av Beth Din* (Head of the Rabbinical Court). Cosgrove represented the older, established community which was readier to make compromises in its Jewish observance while Gottlieb emphasised religious authority as rabbi of what became, in the first post-war decades, the leading synagogue in the city.

Like Rabbi Daiches in Edinburgh, Cosgrove was seen as a Jewish representative to the non-Jewish world, articulate and personable, while Gottlieb stood for the continuation of religious Orthodoxy, while being open to the intellectual challenges facing religion. Chaim Bermant recounted the dispute in his writings, pointing to the failed mediation attempts and describing, with mordant humour, prevailing community attitudes. By the time that the two men had passed away the Glasgow community was very different. Religious leadership and observance came to be based in Giffnock and the synagogues in the Gorbals, Pollokshields, Crosshill and eventually Queens Park itself were to close. Garnethill, however, resisted the demographic changes celebrating its 125th anniversary in 2004 with some hope for the future. It has also been the base for the Scottish Jewish Archives Centre whose expanding records and displays attract a constant stream of academics and visitors.

With a community infrastructure appropriate to much greater numbers the Glasgow Jewish community is faced with the need for rationalisation to adjust to the new demographic realities. Thus organisational closures and Jewish welfare bodies reaching out beyond the community have become part of Glasgow Jewish strategy. The Jewish primary school in Glasgow, Calderwood Lodge, has seen a drop in its school roll but numbers have been buoyant enough for East Renfrewshire Council to plan to move the school to a campus in Newton Mearns, to be shared with a Catholic primary school, by 2017. Edinburgh too has a synagogue too large for its current membership and community concerns focus on achieving arrangements to suit the various, and sometimes disparate, local organisations.

The 2001 and 2011 Censuses make fascinating reading for Jewish Scots. While there is always an element of Jewish under-reporting in Census figures Gillian Raab has pointed out, in issue 74 of the *Edinburgh Star* that the value of the Census is not in absolute numbers but looking at the trends over time. The numbers, as recorded, show a decline in the number of Jews living

Graphic illustration of Jewish population changes between the 2001 and 2011 Censuses. Such Census figures often show under-reporting of Jewish numbers, either because of the voluntary nature of the question or because the concept of belonging implies a level of community attachment difficult for a widely scattered population. (Courtesy Gillian Raab)

		− | +		− | +		− | +
2001	NUMBER 'BELONGING' TO JEWISH RELIGION: 6,448 *of whom were...*	ADDITIONAL JEWS		JEWS BORN		JEWS IMMIGRATED
2001–2010, *during which time...*		UNDECLARED JEWS		JEWS DIED		JEWS EMIGRATED
2011	NUMBER 'BELONGING' TO JEWISH RELIGION: 5,887 (-9%) *resulting in a net change to total...*	-2%		-12%		+5%

in Scotland who see themselves as 'belonging' to the Jewish religion. Some 6,448 Jews were recorded in 2001 but only 5,887 ten years later, a fall of 9%. This compares with a small increase of 1.4% in the number of Jews recorded in the English Census where the question did not include the word 'belonging'. Much of the decline is attributable to the excess of deaths over births in a predominantly older community but the fall was cushioned by the number of Jews moving into Scotland exceeding the number of those leaving.

Thus Scotland was still attracting Jewish immigrants while younger Jewish Scots were in search of a more active Jewish life in London, Manchester, Israel, or even further afield. The demographic shift was seen most starkly in the Glasgow area where the number of Jews fell from 4583 in 2001 to just 3679 in 2011. In contrast the number of Jews in the greater Edinburgh area actually increased by a fifth during this period, from 1036 to 1239. The Jews in the Glasgow area had made up more than 70% of Scotland's Jews in 2001 but the later Census showed that this had fallen to just over 62%, possibly because most of the newcomers had settled in the east of the country. By 2011 there were more than 400 Israelis living in Scotland and others had moved north from a variety of places in England augmented by arrivals from South Africa and Eastern Europe. Prominent newcomers included Lev and Julia Atlas who hailed from Glasgow's twin city of Rostov-on-Don. They were quickly associated with the Jewish community in Glasgow and Lev, a talented violinist and, in 2016, principal viola at the Scottish Opera Orchestra is also a Senior Lecturer in Strings at the Royal Conservatoire of Scotland. He has a PhD (2013) on Russian Chamber Music jointly from the University of St Andrews and the Royal Conservatoire of Scotland. Lev's encyclopaedic knowledge of Jewish klezmer music has made him a popular performer at many Jewish events while Julia's Russian themed restaurant Kossachok serves both as a Russian arts centre and a place where diners could find traditional, though not kosher, Eastern European fare.

Sculptor-mechanic Eduard Bersudsky and theatre director Tatyana Jakovskaya founded *Sharmanka* (Russian for Barrel-Organ) in St. Petersburg in 1989. It has been based in Glasgow since 1996 and audiences in many countries have been fascinated by its magic and fantasy. They had thought to settle in Israel but were told that 'Israel is a small country that cannot cope with

Sharmanka's kinetic theatre art is 'composed of found objects, light and music. Now based in Glasgow, Eduard Bersudsky described one of his works was 'a symbol of Jewish survival in an unstable world.'

one more talented Russian Jew'. His work can be found in such places as Falkirk, Tobermory and the Royal Museum of Scotland in Edinburgh and further afield in Copenhagen, Warsaw and the Bloomfield Science Museum in Jerusalem. Bersudsky won a Creative Scotland Award in 2005.

Concerns about Jewish survival, and the maintenance and transmission of a Jewish heritage in an open society, are almost as old as Jewish history itself. Assimilation and inter-marriage remain challenges to the continuation of the Jewish story in Scotland. Professor Bernard Wasserstein has predicted the disappearance of the Jewish diaspora in Europe 'as a population group, as a cultural entity, and as a significant force in European society'. However, Jews have proved to be remarkably resilient and gloomy future predictions have often not come to pass. The demographic changes may confirm a community in transition but Scotland's Jews have a proud record over the past two centuries and there is much to look forward to in the future.

13 Conclusion

The story of Scotland's Jews reflects the life of a community that within a few decades transformed itself from an immigrant society into an integral part of Scottish life. Scotland proved to be tolerant to the newcomers and the Jewish achievements we have described illustrate that acceptance. Real people formed the human capital in which the Jewish community invested, in their new life in Scotland. We can understand that the demographic changes over the past few decades that we have described are likely to continue and thus will influence the future of Scotland's Jews. However, we have also noted that while the numbers of Jews in Scotland have been declining the loss is being partially mitigated by the movement of Jews into the country, some from England, and what may seem paradoxical, from Israel too. The Jewish population of Scotland may be smaller in the future and perhaps less inclined to see themselves as part of established Jewish organisations but may be more prepared to tap into Jewish activities and events as they present themselves. Jews have proved to be a remarkably resilient people throughout their history and the Jews of Scotland are not about to disappear.

With the aid of detailed information from this study we have been able to analyse trends in population movements, growth, settlement and dispersal in greater detail than previously possible. Previous historical studies have suffered from the difficulties posed by the necessity for time-consuming manual extraction of Jewish data from Census records. These studies were naturally focussed on the specific areas where Jewish concentrations made the search worthwhile, and these were only to be found in Glasgow and to a lesser extent in Edinburgh. In this study, using online information, it has been possible to extend the search to every area through the whole of Scotland. In this concluding chapter we summarise some of the study highlights noting the way these figures match trends in population growth, employment and community attachment.

Alarmed by a rise in anti-Semitic incidents in Scotland, following events in the Middle East in 2014, SCoJeC produced an analysis of the situation, with Scottish Government support, and organised a range of events around the country to bring the community together.

While valuable information was obtained in earlier studies this study has identified material which complements and confirms existing knowledge or even permits its revision. The methodology employed in this study, using the presence of typical Jewish names, places of origin and areas of settlement, has been strengthened by the ability to conduct true nationwide searches following families through several generations. Census data has been checked against communal records and birth, marriage and death registers. While errors in identification, record taking and information gathering in the original documentation remain a problem this study had reduced these to a minimum. Unfortunately, many of the early records are incomplete. Some births are not recorded properly or missed altogether but confidence levels for these figures after 1861 is over 90%. However, we can be sure in saying that between 1861 and 1871 Scotland's Jews doubled in numbers, from 450 to 900, and almost doubled again to 1,619 in 1881 and 3,179 ten years later.

While no-one can claim complete accuracy in such studies we feel confident that real conclusions can be drawn from this work which affect the way that the Jewish experience in Scotland is understood. The study has given us a realistic growth pattern for the Jews in Scotland throughout the 19th century while indicating that Scotland was the first choice of final destination for only a minority of Jewish emigrants from Eastern Europe who passed through the country between 1880 and 1914.

Besides the collection of data relating to migration, settlement and dispersal the study has expanded our knowledge of the first communities in Edinburgh and Glasgow through access to recently digitised records, maps and newspaper reports. This information identifies the first community rabbis, records communal disputes and indicates the precise sites of the small early Edinburgh synagogues.

We have seen how Scottish Jewish communities were often slow to declare the formal, and necessarily public, establishment of a Hebrew Congregation, the title taken by all official Jewish bodies in Scotland's towns and cities. Thus, in Glasgow and Edinburgh, Aberdeen and Dundee, and in the other small communities, synagogues had often been in existence for a number of years avoiding public exposure through concerns about possible expressions of prejudice in the wider population.

At the Census in 1841 we noted that around 40% of Scotland's Jews, then numbering some 323 persons, had been born in Scotland. As statutory birth registration only began in Scotland in 1855 there cannot be complete certainty regarding the earliest data but nevertheless we can see that, in most decades between 1841 and 1881, this figure, of around 40% of the community who had been born in Scotland, remained fairly constant. We have also noted the fluid nature of the early community. In 1851 less than one third of the Jews who had been recorded in Scotland a decade earlier were still there. This pattern was noted also in subsequent Censuses. An interesting statistic which confirms the mobility of the Jewish population in Scotland, and perhaps also the high mortality figures for the period, is that there were only fourteen Jews over the age of 46 years, that is born before the beginning of statutory birth registration in 1855, still living in Scotland in 1901.

Births registered to Jewish families reached 100 in 1887 and doubled just five years later. However, the 1901 Census records just a hundred Jewish children born in Scotland ten years earlier. Given what we now know about the numbers moving out of Scotland from one Census to the next we can confidently say that most of the drop in numbers relates to onward migration and only to a lesser extent the contemporary high levels of child mortality.

One important aspect of the study has been the mapping of the places of marriage, and thus the previous locations, for the Jews living in Scotland. During the course of the nineteenth century most of the marriages of couples who later settled in Scotland took place in present-day Poland, Lithuania and some also in Latvia. Following the expulsion of Jews from Moscow and St. Petersburg in 1891 and the generally unsettled conditions in the Ukraine the geographical spread of migrants became much wider, though the great majority still hailed from Poland and Lithuania.

Decade	Births	Marriages	Deaths	Natural Population Change
1910	3698	836	1094	+2604
1920	2621	1125	1104	+1517
1930	1971	1255	1320	+651
1940	2125	1671	1701	+424
1950	1708	935	1571	+137
1960	1311	823	1657	-346
1970	1004	714	1647	-643
1980	784	480	1561	-777
1990	577	371	1437	-860
2000	323	328	1082	-759

Jewish Births, Marriages, Deaths 1910-2000. The final column indicates the natural population change for the decade. Peak figures for births, marriages and deaths occurred during the 1940s but natural decline did not start until the 1960s. (Courtesy Michael Tobias)

Twentieth Century Trends

By the beginning of the twentieth century the Jewish population in Scotland becomes more settled. From just over 9,000 Jews in 1901 it grew to an estimated 12,000 in 1911. The young population with its comparatively high birth rate and low death rate would have ensured that natural growth would more than compensate for the level of continuing onward migration and community numbers which must have grown until the 1930s and then remained fairly constant for at least two decades.

Most of the transmigrants crossing Britain, rather than sailing directly to their final destinations in North America from a Continental port, did so because of the competitive prices. Following the decline in Hamburg to Leith sailings in the two decades before the First World War most of the passengers crossed the North Sea to Hull or Grimsby. Shipping and rail companies offered integrated travel, often with trains waiting near the port to take onward bound passengers to Liverpool, but also in still significant numbers to Glasgow. The numbers of migrants heading to Glasgow peaked in 1906 and 1907, due to the success of the Allan Line in securing additional migrants for the Glasgow to Canada transmigration route. Jewish passengers, who were not well served with kosher food in steerage accommodation, would also have had the opportunity to replenish their supplies before the longer Atlantic crossing.

Immigrant Occupations

The study examined the occupations of the Jews living in Glasgow from 1841. Not all Census respondents gave details of their work and some entries listed 'not known' or even 'of independent means'. In the early records the predominant occupations were described as merchants or agents, usually dealing in goods demanded by Glasgow's developing middle class, clothing, furs and jewellery. In 1861 there are a number of watchmakers but from 1871 the pattern changes. Migration trends bring a number of Jews engaged in what was often described as typical ghetto trades, above all in tailoring. Thus, tailoring becomes the dominant occupation from 1881 though we have noted how for a short time around 1891 that there is a major move into occupations associated with the tobacco industry with almost a fifth of the Glasgow Jews occupied in this way.

The development of peddling or hawking as a means of making business contacts and establishing the possibility of setting up in business, whether in Glasgow or beyond became a common form of occupation from 1881. Pedlars could start businesses with a minimum both of capital and of risk. Amongst the Jewish residents of the Gorbals in 1881 more than a quarter were involved in hawking and peddling and ten years later their numbers exceeded that of the tailors. The number of Jewish pedlars, hawkers or travellers in Glasgow numbered 541 in 1911 indicating the persistence and endurance of this precarious way of life.

There were no less than five Jewish glaziers in the Gorbals, not often thought of as a Jewish occupation. The list of Jewish master tailors in Glasgow in 1889, supplied by Julius Pinto to the House of Lords Select Committee on the Sweating System, contained twenty-eight names of whom about half were based in the Gorbals. Small shop-keeping in the Gorbals becomes significant by

1891. About a third of the shops are butchers, bakers and grocers and likely to have been supplying kosher food to the Jewish population. General merchants and traders associated with picture frames, manufacturing and selling, are numerous in the first decades of the great migration from Eastern Europe from 1881, but numbers decline as the twentieth century progressed.

The study's detailed analysis of Jewish births, marriages and deaths has enabled an accurate assessment of settlement, growth and subsequent contraction. Keeping strictly to figures where the records can definitely be identified as Jews we can see the remarkable growth in the number of Jewish births through the last half of the 19th century. While only 106 births could be identified during the 1850s the number had grown to 583 during the 1870s on the eve of the great migration. Twenty years later, during the 1890s, there were 2,785 births, reaching a peak a decade later, between 1900 and 1909 when there were no less than 4,576 births. We should recall that during Victorian times childhood infections caused many deaths and these figures do not indicate the whole scope of contemporary demographic change. Childhood mortality was all too frequent and could claim upwards of 10% of all births. While the proportion of child deaths dropped during the first decades of the twentieth century it was only in the 1940s that such deaths became a rarer event, virtually disappearing in subsequent decades. However, health parameters were always better within the Jewish community, even within the first generation to settle in Scotland. Dietary studies showed a better awareness of good food practices, and low levels of alcohol consumption resulting in lower infant mortality than in the wider local population.

From the first decade of the twentieth century we have noted that despite onward migration and the movement of Scottish Jews to England the Jewish population was growing through natural increase. However, in the post-World War II period, and especially during the 1970s, the community aged and the number of deaths peaked. Following the Second World War the baby boomer era stabilised the number of Jewish births and maintained community numbers for a couple of decades. Thereafter, the trend of falling births resumed and community numbers began to decrease. More Jewish school-leavers were entering higher education and setting a trend to study in such English cities as Manchester and Leeds. Few returned to set up homes and indeed many of the marriages represented couples where one Jewish partner was from outside Scotland and the newlyweds settled in England. Jewish births fell precipitately during the 1990s falling to only 323 during the first decade of the twenty-first century. While the number of deaths was also beginning to fall it was clear that demographic decline, irrespective of population movement, was speeding up.

Twenty-first Century

The addition of a religion question to recent Censuses provides interesting information on Jewish population trends in Scotland and invites comparisons with these earlier figures, representing the period of community formation and development. There are of course limitations to what we can learn. Firstly, response to the question was voluntary and further the question in Scotland asked to what religion people belonged and in many parts of Scotland there is no organised community to which they can belong. Further, many Jews remain reticent about answering the religion question and anecdotal evidence tends to match the experience in Canada where around a third of respondents indicate that they are Jewish by ethnicity and not by religion.

In the 2001 Scottish Census, an additional question was asked enquiring about the religion in which people had been brought up. This indicated that on census night while there were 5661 people who were recorded as currently Jewish and brought up Jewish, there were a further 787 people who were currently Jewish but brought up in some other or no religion and 1785 people who were brought up Jewish but either indicated that they had no (774) or another (620) religion or did not answer the religion question (391). These figures have clear implications for the future of the Jewish story in Scotland.

Council Areas	2001	2011	% Change
East Renfrewshire	3128	2399	-23%
Glasgow and surroundings*	1455	1280	-8%
Edinburgh Fife and Lothians	1036	1239	+20%
Elsewhere in Scotland	829	969	+9%
All Scotland	6448	5887	-9%

Source: www.scotlandscensus.gov.uk/en/news/articles/release2a.html (Courtesy Gillian Raab)

Nevertheless, the 2011 Census shows some interesting trends. There are more Israelis in Scotland, now numbering around 400, and the proportion of Scottish Jews in the greater Glasgow area has fallen to 62% the lowest proportion since the middle of the nineteenth century. Those living outside commuting distance of the four cities which still have synagogues has increased to around 9%. At the same time the Jewish population of the Edinburgh and the East of Scotland area has increased (see table above), although part of this increase may be due to Jewish students studying at Scottish universities.

Using data from the Scottish Longitudinal Study that links individuals across Censuses we are able to understand what has contributed to the decrease in the numbers of Scotland's Jews over these ten years. The excess of deaths over births reduces the numbers by 12% and a further 2% decrease comes from people who no longer identify as Jewish, compared to those who do so in 2011. But this is balanced by a 5% increase due to more Jews arriving in Scotland during those 10 years compared to those leaving. Jews are still a more mobile group than the rest of the Scottish population.

In the immigrant period only a little more than ten families were needed to establish a community, often with a synagogue and minister. Today, with many more Jews in outlying areas, there has been no move to establish religious communities but rather a desire to maintain an informal Jewish network. The outreach work by the Scottish Council of Jewish Communities has fostered a sense of community among the Jewish individuals scattered over the length and breadth of the country.

This study has enabled us to understand in more detail the processes by which the Jewish community in Scotland was formed, settled and grew. This book has tried to show how the demographic changes produced the story that has been described in these pages, a story that is informed by the statistics but perhaps even more by the real people and events behind the numbers. As more people around the world look to understand their roots, the place of Scotland as a place of migration and, for many, onward travel carries an increasing resonance. Thus, the story benefits from the reminiscences and artefacts of the newcomers as well as from the personal and Census details.

The Jewish story in Scotland reflects more than just population movements, migration and settlement. We have seen how the professions, business and arts in Scotland benefitted from the Jewish newcomers and have used the stories of people whose lives exemplified the opportunities that Scotland offered. The experiences of the rabbis, cantors and other synagogue officials who served the religious communities from Inverness to Scotland's Central Belt illustrate commitment and care, traditional learning and, in most cases, an accommodation to modernity. Jewish history has produced many examples of transience in many countries. Jewish life in Scotland is of comparatively recent origin but its story tells of a community which became rooted in its new context, contributing to its cultural and professional life in a quantity belying its numbers.

Selected Bibliography

HISTORY

Nathan Abrams,
*Caledonian Jews: A Study of
Seven Small Jewish Communities in Scotland.*
Jefferson, NC and London, 2009

Ben Braber,
Jews in Glasgow 1879-1939 Immigration and Integration,
London, 2007

Gathering the Voices,
testimonies of Kindertransport children and Holocaust survivors who
settled in Scotland can be accessed at:
www.gatheringthevoices.com

Kenneth Collins, Harvey Kaplan, Stephen Kliner,
Jewish Glasgow: A Pictorial History,
Glasgow, 2013

Kenneth Collins (editor)
Aspects of Scottish Jewry,
Glasgow 1987

Kenneth Collins,
*Go and Learn: The International Story of the Jews and Medicine in
Scotland 1739-1945,*
Aberdeen, 1988

HISTORY

Kenneth Collins,
Second City Jewry: The Jews of Glasgow in the Age of Expansion,
Glasgow, 1990

Kenneth Collins,
Be Well! Jewish Immigrant Health and Welfare in Glasgow 1860-1920,
East Linton, 2001

Harvey L Kaplan,
The Gorbals Jewish Community in 1901,
Glasgow, 2006

Abraham Levy,
The Origins of Glasgow Jewry 1812-1895,
Glasgow, 1949

Abraham Levy,
The Origins of Scottish Jewry,
London, 1958

Viki McDonnell,
Greenock's Jewish Community: 1880-1940,
Greenock, 2012

Abel Phillips,
A History of the Origins of the First Jewish Community in Scotland: Edinburgh 1816,
Edinburgh, 1979

Mark Smith,
Treblinka Survivor: the Life and Death of Hershl Sperling,
Stroud, 2010

Michael Tobias,
A Study of 19th Century Scottish Jewry,
MSc thesis, University of Strathclyde, Glasgow 2012

Thomas Toughill,
Oscar Slater: the Mystery Solved,
Edinburgh, 2011

MEMOIRS

Chaim Bermant, *Coming Home,* London, 1976

Jenni Calder, *Not Nebuchadnezzar,* Edinburgh, 2005

Evelyn Cowan,
Spring Remembered: A Scottish Jewish Childhood,
Penicuik, 1974

David Daiches,
Two Worlds: An Edinburgh Jewish Childhood,
Edinburgh, 1971, 1997

David Daiches, *Was: A Pastime from Time Past,* London, 1975

Howard Denton & Jim C Wilson, *The Happy Land,* Edinburgh, 1991

Ralph Glasser, *Growing up in the Gorbals,* London, 1986

Ralph Glasser, *Gorbals Boy at Oxford,* London, 1988

Ralph Glasser, *Gorbals Voices, Siren Songs,* London, 1990

Edith Hofman,
Mackerel at Midnight- Growing up Jewish on a Remote Scottish Island,
Philadelphia, 2005

Albert Jacob,
The Day it Hit the Fan: Memoirs of a Reluctant Politician,
Israel, 2005

Ernest Levy, *The Single Light,* Edgeware, Middx., 2007

Ernest Levy, *Just One More Dance,* Edinburgh, 1998

Rosa Sacharin,
The Unwanted Jew: A Struggle for Acceptance,
e-book 2014

Benno Schotz, *Bronze in My Blood,* Edinburgh, 1981

ART

Fiona Frank,
Hannah Frank – a Glasgow Artist: Drawings and Sculpture,
Glasgow, 2004

Hilda Goldwag's Glasgow,
Collins Gallery Exhibition Catalogue,
Glasgow

Marianne Grant,
*I knew I was Painting for My Life:
the Holocaust Artworks of Marianne Grant*,
Deborah Haase (editor)
Glasgow, 2002

FICTION

Chaim Bermant, *Jericho Sleep Alone*, London, 1964

Chaim Bermant, *Ben Preserve Us*, London, 1965

Chaim Bermant, *The Second Mrs Whitberg*, London, 1976

Chaim Bermant, *The Patriarch*, London, 1976

Jack Ronder, *The Lost Tribe*, London, 1981

J David Simons, *The Credit Draper*, Ullapool, 2008

J David Simons, *The Liberation of Celia Kahn*, Nottingham, 2011

C P Taylor, *Bread and Butter*, Harmondsworth, 1967

C P Taylor, *Walter*, Edinburgh, 1992

Glossary

Most Hebrew and Yiddish terms should be clear from the context.
The following may also be helpful.

Aliyah: Literally 'ascent'. Used as a description of being 'called up' to reading from the Torah in the synagogue and of 'ascending upwards' to settle in the Land of Israel.

Beth Din: Jewish court of law, dealing mainly with issues related to kosher food and personal status, e.g. religious divorces *(get, pl. gittin)*.

Chanukah: Eight-day winter festival of lights recalling the struggle of the Maccabees to free the land of Israel and restore the Temple in Jerusalem.

Chazzan: Synagogue cantor responsible for leading the services.

Chuppah: Literally 'marriage canopy'. Jewish couples are married under the *chuppah* whether in the synagogue or out of doors.

Der Heim: (Literally, 'the homeland). The Yiddish term for the western area of the Russian Empire, usually referred to as the Pale of Settlement, which was the permitted region of Russia where Jews were allowed to settle.

Froom: Religiously observant (Yiddish).

Kosher: Food prepared in accordance with Jewish law. Includes meat and poultry produced by **shechita**, and the separation of meat and milk. Many kosher products carry the logo of a rabbinic authority **(hechsher)** to certify that the product is *kosher*.

Landsman: Persons now settled in their new communities but hailing from the same town in Eastern Europe.

Midrash: Collection of rabbinic legends.

Mikva: Ritual bath used monthly by married women, by converts to Judaism on their acceptance into the faith and by men on the eve of Sabbath and holy days.

Minyan: Prayer quorum of ten men above the age of 13 years *(bar mitzvah)*.

Mishnayot: Collections of rabbinic tradition and lore forming the Mishna. With its commentary, the Gemara, it forms the Talmud.

Mohel: Religious functionary trained to carry out religious circumcisions *(brit milah)* usually on the eighth day of a baby boy's life.

Rabbi: Teacher and spiritual leader of the community. The rabbi answers questions on Jewish law, gives sermons and performs the duties of a minister of religion. Many of the synagogue ministers in Scotland were qualified to act as *shochet* or *mohel* but did not have the rabbinical certificate *(semichah)*.

Rebbe: Rabbi, usually of the pietistic Hassidic movement

Sefer Torah: The Torah scroll contains the Five Books of Moses handwritten by a skilled scribe on parchment. Portions are read on an annual cycle on Sabbaths and also on Monday, Thursday and Festivals mornings.

Shabbat / Shabbos (Sabbath): The weekly day of rest beginning with dusk on Friday and ending with full darkness on Saturday night. The Sabbath represents a day of rest from all creative activity, and religious codes describe Sabbath practice. Thus, it is a time for synagogue prayer and home-based activities such as family meals.

Shochet: Religious functionary who has been trained to carry out *shechita*, the Jewish method for the rapid and painless killing of kosher animals for food.

Shteible: Small synagogue, conventicle.

Shtetl: Small Eastern European town with a significant Jewish population.

Yarmulke: Yiddish for skullcap, also known as *kipa* in Hebrew. Traditional head covering worn by Jewish adult males during prayers and frequently all day.

Yeshiva: Religious school (seminary) – often providing full-time secondary level education in Jewish texts.

Index

G

H

I

R

S

T

V

W

Y

Z